PORTRAIT
OF A
MINORITY

ASIANS IN EAST AFRICA

PORTRAIT
OF A
MINORITY

ASIANS IN EAST AFRICA

Edited by
DHARAM P. GHAI

Nairobi
OXFORD UNIVERSITY PRESS
London   New York
1965

Oxford University Press, Amen House, London E.C.4

GLASGOW NEW YORK TORONTO MELBOURNE WELLINGTON
BOMBAY CALCUTTA MADRAS KARACHI LAHORE DACCA
CAPE TOWN SALISBURY NAIROBI IBADAN ACCRA
KUALA LUMPUR HONG KONG

Cover design by
BERYL MOORE

Printed and bound in Nairobi by
East African Printers, Kenya, Ltd.

Contents

Acknowledgements

In the course of editing this book, I have received help, in one form or another, from a large number of persons. It is not possible to mention them all by name. However, I should like to acknowledge publicly my debt to certain individuals who have been especially helpful. I am indebted to Charles Richards and Roger Houghton of Oxford University Press for making a special effort to bring the book out in what must be a record time. My thanks are also due to Winifred da Silva for secretarial assistance. Professor Raymond Apthorpe, Miss Krishna Ahooja, Ralph Tanner, Emil Rado and Sarjit Heyer read parts of the manuscript and made valuable comments. My greatest debt, however, is to Professor Terence Ranger who read through the entire draft manuscript and made extensive and detailed comments, which have resulted in a substantial improvement in the book.

Finally, I must express my deep gratitude to my brother Yash who read the proofs and helped in a thousand other ways, and to my wife Neela who, apart from taking a keen interest in the project, has been an unfailing source of encouragement and help.

Makerere University College   Dharam Ghai
June, 1965

Contributors

DHARAM GHAI was born in Kenya, where he received his secondary education at the Duke of Gloucester School, Nairobi. He went to Oxford in 1955 to read for an honours degree in Philosophy, Politics and Economics and stayed on to complete his B.Phil. (Econ.). In 1959 he was awarded a fellowship to work for a doctorate in Economics at Yale University. He returned to East Africa in 1961 to take up a lectureship in Economics at Makerere University College. He has written extensively on development problems of the East African countries, and has just completed a book on 'Taxation and Economic Growth in Uganda.' He has also been a consultant to the governments of Uganda and Buganda on economic problems.

CHANAN SINGH was born in India, but came to work for the Railways Administration in Kenya in 1923. He studied privately to obtain a bachelor's degree in Economics from London University and was also called to the Bar. For several years he practised as a barrister. In the course of a long and distinguished public career, he has held many important posts, having been the Secretary of the Kenya Indian Congress, founder of the Kenya Freedom Party, President of the Nairobi Indian Association, and the President of the Law Society of Kenya. He was a member of the Legislative Council of Kenya from 1952 to 1956, and 1960 to 1964. He was Parliamentary Secretary to the Prime Minister of Kenya before being appointed to his present position as a Judge of the Supreme Court in 1964.

AGEHANANDA BHARATI was born in Austria. He embraced Hinduism at an early age. He received his education at Vienna University, and is now a leading specialist on Asian, especially Indian, culture and civilization. He spent several years in India, during which he travelled extensively and mastered six Indian languages, including Sanskrit. He is the author of several books on Indian religion and civilization, and has also written numerous articles in learned journals on anthropology, religion and philosophy. He visited East Africa in 1964 to collect material for a sociological study of

Asians in East Africa. He is currently Professor of Indian Studies at Syracuse University in the United States.

YASH TANDON was born in Uganda in 1939. After receiving his school education at Mbale Secondary School, he studied at the London School of Economics from 1958 to 1964, where he took a B.Sc. degree, specializing in international relations. He is just completing his doctoral dissertation on the United Nations Peace Commissions. He has written articles on international affairs and has been lecturing in the same field at Makerere University College since July, 1964.

PIYARALLY RATTANSI was born in Kenya and studied at the Duke of Gloucester School in Nairobi. He spent several years at the London School of Economics, where he took both his bachelor's degree and his doctorate. He was for two years a Research Fellow in the Department of Philosophy at Leeds University and is now a lecturer there. His main field of specialization is the history and philosophy of science. He has attended several international conferences and written articles on the philosophy of science.

MOHAMMED ABDULLA was born in India where he took an honours degree in history at Agra University. He has been teaching history at the Duke of Gloucester School in Nairobi since 1951. He went to U.K. in 1962 on a Kenya Government scholarship to study for a master's degree in Education at Durham University.

YASH GHAI was born in Kenya in 1938. After receiving his education at the Duke of Gloucester School, Nairobi, he went on to Oxford, *via* Royal College, Nairobi, to take an honours degree in Jurisprudence. In 1961 he was elected to a Nuffield College studentship and the following year was awarded a fellowship at the Harvard Law School. He was called to the Bar in 1963. He has been a lecturer in Law at the University College, Dar es Salaam since August, 1963. He has written articles in legal journals on international and constitutional law, and is currently working on a book on the laws and constitution of Kenya. He is also completing a doctoral dissertation for Oxford University on 'The Protection of Minorities in International Law and Commonwealth Constitutions.'

Introduction

Dharam P. Ghai

This symposium owes its origin to a realization that very little of importance has been written on the life and problems of the Asian community in East Africa.* In the past the racial problems of the East African countries have tended to be seen as mainly those of European/African relations. There is consequently a long and lively literature on the Europeans in East Africa. The relative paucity of written material on Asians is in no small measure due to the lack of local Asian scholarship.

It is now becoming increasingly clear that the place of the Asians in the new emerging societies of East Africa constitutes the dominant problem in the field of race relations. There is, therefore, an urgent need for a sympathetic but detached and realistic treatment of the problems and predicament of the Asian community. The present volume is an attempt in this direction.

All but one of the contributors to this symposium are Asians who were either born or have lived most of their working lives in East Africa. The present volume is not, however, intended, in any sense, to represent an Asian point of view; although the fact that these essays are written by Asians must invest them with greater interest and realism. The purpose of the book is to give a comprehensive picture of the Asian community in all its facets, and to analyse its problems and prospects at a crucial stage in its history. The book has no message for the Asian community: its approach is analytical rather than didactic or laudatory. In so far as it focuses on Asians as an alien minority, it is hoped that it will be of wider interest to students of problems of minorities in plural societies.

The present volume consists of six studies: the first, giving the historical background necessary for an understanding of the later

---

*Practically all of them are of Indian and Pakistani origin. The term 'Asian' came into use after the partition of India, as the more accurate 'Indian' was no longer acceptable to the Muslims. 'Asian' is used here to conform with current usage. It does not include the Arabs, for example.

studies, is followed by social, political, economic and educational surveys. The last chapter, in many ways the most crucial, draws on the earlier chapters to present an analysis of the future prospects of Asians in East Africa. All symposia suffer from some inherent defects: the present one is no exception. Some of the studies overlap in their themes and are, therefore, necessarily repetitious. The contributors, in most cases, did not have access to other studies at the time of writing. This probably accounts for the variety of standpoints from which these essays are written. However, it was decided to publish them as they were written, without any major changes, in order mainly to preserve the sense of unity within each essay, but also to present different strands of opinion on some of the complex and controversial themes treated in this volume. If this work succeeds in stirring up a serious discussion of the role of the Asian community in a new and rapidly changing East Africa, it will have surpassed the expectations of its authors.

1. The Historical Background

Chanan Singh*

For over two thousand years Indians were at the heart of the economic activity which brought the influences of a wider world to the East coast of Africa. Indians rarely controlled the great oceanic trade routes and never controlled politically or militarily the East African coast itself. But throughout the period, whoever governed the coast and its hinterland and whoever dominated the Indian Ocean, India remained the most important market for East African goods and the most important source of the trade goods which were exchanged for them. East African gold and ivory and slaves poured into India over the centuries; and into East Africa there poured in return Indian cloth and beads, Indian skill and capital. For it was never merely a matter of others, acting as middlemen, exchanging goods between Africa and India; there were always Indian merchants, financiers, sailors, pilots.

Of all the peoples who were at one time or another involved in the East African trade, indeed, the Indians showed themselves the most persistent and the most resilient. In times of economic prosperity, when the whole Indian Ocean trade complex was booming, Indians throve in the East African trade. But in times of economic disruption, when old trading systems were being shattered by the advent of new political powers, whether Portuguese, German or British, Indians were still in demand for their skills and labour. Neutrals in the great struggle between Christianity and Islam, the Hindu merchants and traders especially were able to continue their activities along the East African coast throughout the whole period.

The process was first recorded in the 'Periplus of the Erythrean Sea', a Greek guide for sailors compiled around A.D. 100. Marco Polo retailed stories about Indian links with Africa centuries later; later still the Portuguese, as they forced their way round Africa

---

*The author was Parliamentary Secretary to the Prime Minister of Kenya when he wrote this paper. He is now a Judge of the Supreme Court of Kenya.

into the Indian Ocean, found the ancient Indian commerce with East Africa at one of its most prosperous peaks. They found ports crowded with Indian ships; a great East African demand for Indian goods which in the end forced the newcomers to deal in such goods themselves instead of attempting to compete with the products of Portugal: Indian settlements; Indian pilots. There is nothing, indeed, to indicate that Indians had penetrated into the interior or made contact with its Bantu state systems. But on the coast they were playing a key economic role.

The Portuguese attack upon the Moslem controlled economic system of the Indian Ocean and the consequent disruption of the East coast trade was the first of the great crises faced by the Asians in East Africa. In the sixteenth and seventeenth centuries the prosperity of the whole coast was sapped and as opportunity declined, so too did Indian participation. But the Indian link was not broken. Trading links with India continued to the north of Portuguese settlement, and within the area of Portuguese control Indian activity and influence even developed new forms. For the Portuguese, after all, their East African possessions and tributaries were part of a great Oceanic empire of which Goa was the economic, administrative and cultural centre. In a real sense the East African coast became a province of an Indian administration and Indians, especially Goans, were soon actively involved in Portuguese penetration and development. Indian labour was used to construct forts along the coast. Indian traders and adventurers and junior administrators took part in the chequered process of penetration into the interior. By the nineteenth century Asians were an informal advance guard of Portuguese influence in Central Africa; Asian traders operated every season in the gold areas of Mashonaland; Goan adventurers, of whom Gouveia was the best known, carved out virtual personal empires for themselves on the western borders of the Portuguese colony.

Something of the same pattern can be seen with the coming of German and British imperial rule in East Africa. In the first part of the nineteenth century the coast north of Mozambique experienced a striking revival of economic prosperity under the influence of the Omani Arabs and particularly of Sultan Seyyid Said. Basing himself on Zanzibar, the shrewd merchant prince built up a commercial empire and his subjects pushed deep into East Africa in the interests of a booming trade in ivory and slaves. European and North African markets were perhaps the key ones in this trade but Indian participation was as vital as ever. Seyyid

Said made explicit and successful efforts to involve Indian traders, administrators and financiers in his ventures. They did not participate on any scale in the push into the interior any more than Indians had done before the arrival of the Portuguese but in Zanzibar itself and on the coast their numbers steadily grew. In 1844 it was estimated that there were some 1,200 Asians resident in East Africa; by 1860 there were some 6,000. In Zanzibar the key post of Customs Master was almost always held by an Indian in this period, its holder acting as banker and financial adviser to the Sultan as well as being collector of customs revenue. Indians were the virtual monopolists of retail trade. In 1873 Sir Bartle Frere noted that 'throughout our whole circuit, from Zanzibar round by Mozambique and Madagascar and up to Cape Guardafui, we did not, except at Johanne, meet half a dozen exceptions to the rule that every shopkeeper was an Indian.' Above all, Indians financed and supplied the caravans to the interior.

The coming of the Germans and the British—and of the Free State in the Congo—opened the second instalment of Christian-Muslim contest in East Africa. This time the economic and political interests of Islam suffered a massive overthrow. Zanzibar was cut off from its hinterland; the whole far-flung structure of Arab-Swahili trade was shattered; the caravans suppressed; and European political control established after fierce resistance by the old controllers of East Africa trade had been put down. Once again an economic system in which Asians had been operating profitably was broken. But once again the Asians survived.

As far as the British were concerned it was even more true of them than it had been of the Portuguese that their East African territories were extensions of an Indian empire. The carry-over of ideas from the Indian administrative system to British East Africa was greater even than the old flow between Goa and Mozambique. The Indians who had been participating in the Zanzibar-Swahili trade system had been, in fact, British subjects, and this had been in itself a factor in British expansion on the mainland. The charter of 3 September, 1888, granted by Queen Victoria to the Imperial British East Africa Company, for instance, gave as one of the reasons for official backing of the Company that: 'the possession by a British Company of the coastline, as above defined, and which includes the port of Mombasa, would be advantageous to the commercial and other interests of our subjects in the Indian Ocean, who may otherwise be compelled to reside and trade under the government or protection of alien powers.'

Many of the British officers who came to East Africa during the early days had served the Government of India. Burton and Speke were themselves officers of the Indian army and were provided with instruments and equipment by the Government of India. Indian coinage was made official coinage in East Africa; Indian laws were extended there. Indian troops were imported from time to time to keep order. Just as the Portuguese had used Indian labour to build forts, so the British used Indian labour to build the railway systems of British East Africa. And just as the Portuguese penetration of Mozambique had been followed, or sometimes preceded, by Indian and Goan enterprise, so the establishment of British administration and the opening of the line of rail was followed by a large-scale movement of Indian traders into the interior, long before white settlers in any number arrived. It was little wonder that some Englishmen at least thought of East Africa in terms of an economic dependency of India; envisaged it being exploited through the immigration of Indian peasant farmers; and generally conceived of an Indian development of the area under British control.

In German East Africa, 'under the government or protection of an alien power', natives of British India were in a much less immediately strong position. The Germans made some effort in the early days to break the Indian monopoly of trading activity in their territory by encouraging African enterprise. But the economic facts remained and had to be accepted; in Tanganyika Asians played only slightly less an important economic role than in Kenya.

Up to this point of their connection with East Africa, Indians had rarely taken part in explicitly political activity. Concentrating upon economic enterprise, they had adapted themselves in turn to the indigenous coastal chiefs, to the Arabs, to the Portuguese, to the Arabs again, and now to the British and the Germans. To all these regimes they had been, to a greater or less degree, economically indispensable. But now a new factor began to operate. It was not long before the idea that East Africa was in some way an area providentially set aside for Asian economic enterprise was challenged by the idea that East Africa was a white man's country. The growth of white settler communities in East Africa for the first time offered a fundamental challenge to the economic position of Asians. Between these white settler communities and the Asians there did not exist that alliance of mutual economic benefit which had been struck between the Swahili caravan leaders and the Indian financiers of the 19th century. Instead, a fierce economic rivalry sprang up, most obviously centring on access to land but flowing into many other fields.

It would be wrong, of course, to over-state this situation. Asians, white settlers and Africans managed to co-exist and co-operate economically and Asian attitudes have remained profoundly tinged by the old gospel of co-operation and survival, no matter what the regime. But there were frequent enough threats to the whole economic position of the Asians to drive them into political activity, especially because they saw that the white settler element was using political pressure to achieve economic ends. So in the twentieth century the Asian communities of East Africa, and of Kenya in particular, began to play a part in the political as well as in the economic history of the area.

Once this development had begun the old connection with mainland India began to take on a new significance. For not only were Indians in East Africa driven to political action but at the same time Indians in India itself were developing a newly articulate national sense and building up strong nationalist movements. The interconnections between the two developments were of the utmost importance to the course of East African politics, and just as Britain had been inclined to treat East Africa in the past as an economic dependent of India, so now she had to see East African politics in the context of Indian nationalism.

It will be best to take the Kenyan experience to illustrate these generalizations. In the first days very much use was made of Asians in Kenya; it was planned to introduce Indian peasant settlers; and official British opinion was favourable towards these industrious and valuable subjects. But things soon began to change. From the Governorship of Elliott onwards a policy of discrimination in favour of the white settler came to be adopted. The settlers themselves developed with skill and energy the arts of political pressure; to a varying degree they succeeded in influencing both local administrative officials and British politicians. And it was the aim of the settlers to achieve both political and economic dominance.

As farming developed in Kenya, access to land became one of the main points of controversy. As early as 1902 the Indian Association of Mombasa was protesting about discrimination in land grants, and then received an assurance that there was 'no

intention of drawing a distinction between Europeans and Indians
as far as rights of mining, settling and acquiring land' were concerned. This official policy came under heavy pressure, however.
In 1905 a Commission on land allocation, under the Chairmanship
of the settler leader, Lord Delamere, reported that while there was
'no objection to the general proposition that Indians should hold
land in the Protectorate . . . considering only a small area of the
Protectorate is suitable for European settlement and colonisation,
it is desirable that land within that area should be reserved for the
support and management of a white population.' In July 1906
this pressure was successful; Lord Elgin, Secretary of State for the
Colonies, approved the practice of granting land in the so-called
White Highlands only to European settlers.

This initial settler success was followed up by attempts to deny
Asians the right to own land anywhere in Kenya. In 1907 the
Land Board passed a resolution to that effect; but it proved impossible to carry British opinion to this extent. In 1915, however,
the reservation of land in the Highlands for whites was embodied
in law. And in practice the principle of segregation was also
applied in urban areas through the imposition of racial covenants.

It soon became apparent to the Asian community of Kenya
that if they were to protect themselves against this sort of discriminatory economic competition they must seek some rival source
of local political power and pressure. Thus, not content with
merely lobbying the Aga Khan and Winston Churchill over the
land issue, they raised the issue of the non-European franchise
long before it had become the target of African politicians. The
struggle between the Asian and European communities over
representation was of very considerable importance to Kenya, very
possibly frustrating the white drive to self rule there, and stimulating
African political thinking and activity.

Indian demands for political representation at first met with
some success. Winston Churchill, as Under-Secretary at the
Colonial Office, was an advocate—'There can be no reason for
excluding this large and meritorious class', he minuted. After
an Indian petition in April 1908 it was decided that a representative
of that community should be nominated to the Legislative Council
and in 1909 Mr. A. M. Jeevanjee was selected by Acting Governor
Jackson. But already the counter-tide was running strongly and
the Kenyan Indian community began to appeal to wider audiences.
As early as 1910 they demonstrated their ability to win the sympa-

thies of the Indian national movement. In that year Jeevanjee took his case to London and achieved the support of the All-India Moslem League. Later his statements were printed in India itself with an appeal for the support of Congress and a suggestion that East Africa be annexed formally to the Indian Empire.

So it went on with each white initiative countered by an Asian reaction. War-time demands by whites provoked the founding of the East African Indian National Congress; the success of the whites in gaining a European-only franchise in 1917 provoked the great struggle between themselves and the Asian community in the years immediately following the First World War. These years were marked by white abuse and suspicion of Asians, even by white plans to arrest and deport the leaders of the Asian community. They were marked also by Indian appeals to Britain, to Indian nationalism, to the Government of India. At this time also there came into being the first contacts between Indian and African nationalism; the Indian editor, M. A. Desai, giving publicity in his paper to the grievances of the Kikuyu and allowing Harry Thuku to use his office as a headquarters. At the time there was a tendency to see emergent African politics in the context of the struggle between whites and Asians and to judge the 'loyalty' of Africans in terms of their hostility to Indians. But the links between early African nationalist leaders and Indian nationalism through Asians resident in East Africa, had a significance in the precocious emergence of radical African politics in Kenya which has not yet been fully explored.

Whatever positive contributions Asian politics made to emerging African nationalism in terms of objectives or methods, there is no doubt that negatively Asian activity was of very great importance to the long term results of the struggle between black and white. Because of the Asian community the question of the justice or propriety of white political demands there received altogether wider debate than the similar white aspirations in Rhodesia. While there was no articulate opponent of Southern Rhodesian white demands for self-government, the Government of India constituted itself the formidable advocate of the Kenyan Asian case, and argued point for point with the advocates of white advance. 'Would the settlers now succeed in making Kenya a typical British Colony?', asks George Bennett rhetorically in his *Kenya: A Political History*. 'In this objective they were under challenge from the Indians. It may well be that it was only their rivalry which prevented the Europeans from establishing their position in Kenya as in places further south.' Or again, describing the rebuff delivered to white aspirations with the African paramountcy declaration of 1923, Bennett writes: 'The full weight of this rebuff may be measured against the grant of this same status to the Southern Rhodesian settlers in the same year—but they had no Indians to contend with.'

This was the most significant Asian contribution to the political history of East Africa but it was not the only one. The European rebuff certainly did not mean an Indian victory and the contest between the communities continued. Among the Indian politicians were a handful of radical nationalists of a political sophistication beyond anything possible for African politics at the same date and these men had a significant influence on developing African nationalism. There was Isher Dass, with his policy of boycott and non-cooperation; his opposition to Closer Union moves; his links with the Indian nationalist movements. It was Dass who in the 1939 Legislative Council read into the record the petitions of the African organizations, the Kikuyu Central Association and the Kavirondo Taxpayers' Welfare Association against the Order in Council to define the Highlands. There was Makan Singh, the Sikh trade unionist, who organized the Labour Trade Union of East Africa, established contact with Kikuyu labour leaders, and played a key role in the Mombasa dock strike of 1939.

There is no point, of course, in attempting to over-state this Asian radicalism or their part in opposition politics. There was always an economic and incipient political rivalry between Africans and Asians; and the majority of the Asian community had no desire to associate itself with the radicalism of Makan Singh or Isher Dass. Still, by virtue of the situation in which they found themselves and of the links with Indian nationalism, the Asians did at times speak for the Africans as well as for themselves. One can quote African testimony to this, all the more effective for being obviously reluctant. In the Legislative Council in the late 1940s an African member admitted: 'I never thought that I would ever side with the Indian community as I now do, but I am forced by circumstances and cannot help it. I must therefore say that in this Council the Indian members are more helpful to the African community than the Europeans because they think of what the African community desire.'

The other East African territories had a more peaceful political history than Kenya. Essentially the Asian communities in these territories were faced with precisely the same problems as Kenyan Asians, but racial conflicts were not so acute or defined. In Tanganyika, indeed, with its Trust Territory status, Asians rose to the senior ranks of the civil service and there was less franchisal discrimination.

But there comes out of the history of these other territories the second theme of Asian life in East Africa—a theme which is now the dominant one. We have already said that in Kenya especially the challenge of white economic enterprise drove Asians into political activity. We have remarked also on the incipient political and actual economic competition of Asians and Africans there. In Uganda and Zanzibar this competition was already the major issue in the 1920s and 1930s.

In the long history of Asian economic enterprise in East Africa there had been until the colonial era relatively little contact with the African peoples either in the form of economic collaboration or competition. Asians had mainly been dealing with the various powers who controlled the coast or the ocean trade routes. In particular they had not been concerned with the production of goods, though they had financed their collection; it was their role to trade in the goods produced by others. As Indians went inland under the umbrella of the colonial power they came to play additional economic roles and to assume positions hitherto monopolized by Africans themselves. As various African peoples responded to the new economic opportunities rivalry between them and the Asian business-man and trader was bound to develop. This happened most clearly in Uganda, where the traditional system managed to modify itself successfully; to retain its control of land and production; and to exclude white settlers. The highly material, competitive society of the Baganda entered into the world of modern economic opportunity with zeal. Asians played a significant role in assisting the development of agriculture in Uganda and were especially prominent in the early stages of the cotton industry. But their participation brought them into repeated conflict with African farmers who resented the Asian monopoly of marketing and ginning; and gradually African co-operatives began to act effectively to break down that monopoly. This economic competition created much ill feeling and during the Kenya contest of the early 1920s, the whites were able to produce numerous anti-Asian statements from Uganda Africans to strengthen their case. Any Indian who rested his optimism about Asian relations with Africans on the growing co-operation between them in Kenyan politics would have been well advised to look at Uganda as a corrective. In Uganda the Asians were also meeting with economic competition backed by use of political power; but there was little possibility of countering it.

In Zanzibar a similarly instructive situation developed. Asians had for long occupied posts of importance in the island's administration and continued to do so. Though the break-up of the old economic system reduced the importance of Zanzibar and led to a movement of Asians to the mainland, there still remained considerable Asian investment. Asians had a virtual monopoly of the marketing and export of cloves, which were now the mainstay of the Zanzibar economy. In the 1930s there was a very considerable re-organization of the industry in order to increase the participation of the indigenous population. In this case the Asian merchants attempted to counter with political pressure; they protested to the Indian Government and K.P.S. Menon was sent to examine the situation. But the publication of his report had no impact on the policy of government in Zanzibar and the Indian merchants had to adapt themselves to the new situation.

In various ways, then, the events of the twentieth century, even before the independence revolution, had greatly changed the character of Asian activity in East Africa. With its emphasis upon Asian economic interests this chapter has not perhaps sufficiently brought out the extent to which Asians were steadily ceasing to play a dominant role in East African commerce or development. Significant though their skills and capital remained, more sophisticated skills and much greater capital resources were becoming available from other sources. And this is a picture which has certainly not been modified with independence; neither the Indian Government nor Asians generally now take an important place amongst the suppliers of skills and capital to the independent nations of East Africa. The old Indian Ocean trading complex is no longer an important element in their economic life.

Thus Asians have lost their economic indispensability and they have also become involved in competition with Africans. To protect themselves in this vulnerable position the new tradition of political activity which they developed in Kenya as a retort to white pressures is of little avail to them. The techniques of appeal to India and to the British press cannot be used in the new circumstances. In fact, the old link with India which was for centuries of such vital economic and political significance, has little reality now.

It might be thought that there was little from their long history in East Africa likely to be of use to Asians today. Still, Asians can not unreasonably claim to have contributed something to development over hundreds of years; they can claim also to have shared the common disabilities of white racialism; they can claim to have helped to do something about them. To this extent their history can be used; and of course, whether useful or not, it is still this history which continues to mould and to shape Asian attitudes and actions today.

2. A Social Survey

Agehananda Bharati

The scope of this paper is purely descriptive. It is neither prescriptive nor prophylactic. Audiences in East Africa and in India and Pakistan might be impatient with scholars who deal with Indian society without giving any advice to its members about preferable or expedient behaviour. This cannot be helped, as counselling and edification are not the job of the social anthropologist. Although descriptive, this paper is not statistical. It is based on field-research at the time of its compilation.[1] Statistical material does not seem relevant to the sort of survey here intended.

At the outset, it is necessary to adumbrate the place of the Indian population and its growth in the East African domicile. Of all the ethnic groups resident in East Africa, the Asians have no doubt experienced the largest population increase proportionately. 'Asians' is the East African synonym for all domiciled people of Indian (or Pakistani) origin. The term 'Indian' seems to be applied to guests from India, temporary visitors, Indian government agencies and the people in India—there are no non-Indian 'Asians' present as calculable minority groups in East Africa. The population increase in East Africa is higher than in the parallel linguistic and caste-groups in the Indian homeland. This development, however, has come to a rather sudden halt and during the past decade, but especially since the East African nations achieved their independence, there has been a conscious and widespread attempt to curb the number of children, though there is no concerted effort yet of family planning. Economically more affluent and relatively more sophisticated families are certainly conscious of the necessity of family planning. Upper echelon government servants, business executives, professional people of all linguistic and religious groups, not even with the exception of the Catholic Goans, are cognisant of the fact that scientific birth-control is as important to the settlers in East Africa as it is in India and Pakistan. The only objection to scientific birth-control is voiced by some of the older, tradition-bound Gujarati Hindus who claim that people have many children because they like them, because it adds to the love and affection in the family and 'that it has always been this way,' that God gives children. Some younger puritanical fundamentalists, such as the followers of the *Brha Bharatiya Sangh*, 'the greater India Union', organized on the model of the Hindu Fascist R.S.S. in India or the more radical among the Arya Samajists—a fundamentalistic reform movement founded roughly a century ago in the Panjab— claim that sexual continence (*brahmacharyam*) as taught by Mahatma Gandhi, Swami Dayananda Sarasvati (the founder of the Arya Samaj) and by other teachers of the Hindu religious lore, should be the sole answer to the problem of overpopulation. However, the ubiquitous feeling that the coming generation of Indian settlers does not have much of an economic and social future in East Africa is no doubt the most powerful single factor in the reduction of the birth-rate among the minority in the last few years.

It is as yet hard to say whether the sub-communities as well as the vocations which have a lesser chance of survival through 'Africanization' tend to be more actively conscious of the need of birth-control in their own kin-groups than the sections which write off the possibility of a return to India or Pakistan—I am particularly thinking of the Khoja Ishmailis, the followers of the Aga Khan, who have virtually no place to go 'back' to as they have no substantial communities worth the name in India or Pakistan. The Panjabi communities, Hindu, Sikh, and Sunni and Ahmeddiya Muslims, are the most vulnerable and hence the most insecure, because the majority of them are government employees or attached to governmental and semi-governmental organizations which are likely to replace Asians by indigenous Africans within a short time. The fear possessing most Indians, that the taking out of East African citizenship, as recommended by the official voices of the countries involved, may not eventually help them to preserve their job and their livelihood constitutes the most pervasive anxiety syndrome among all Asian groups, but of course particularly among 'servants'. Even stronger apprehensions are felt by the small *duka* (shop) owners all over East Africa, i.e., by the Gujaratis who have given the image of the Indian as a petty, money-grabbing trader, to both Africans and Europeans in East Africa. These *dukas* (a detailed account of which is given in Dharam Ghai's contribution), owned almost exclusively by Gujarati-speaking Asians, are being crowded out by the African co-operatives and by an increasing boycott from the side of the former African clientele. It is perhaps only the top industrialist and businessman, and the very few large-scale Indian farmers, who would bid for a future successful residence in East Africa.

As seen from what little has been said so far, it is impossible to deal with the Indian minority in East Africa *en bloc;* there is virtually nothing of sociological significance about the minority which would hold for all its constituent groups. Ideally, each of these groups should be dealt with quite separately, for they form more autonomous sub-cultures than, say, the Jews and the Irish in Boston who have been written about in great profusion as distinct sub-cultures. Linguistic and communal divisions, trans-group relations, in-group coherence and the whole range of sociologically diversifying elements must be adduced if a study like this is at all to be seriously attempted. Divisive tendencies in Indian society have been studied by many authors; in the East African region, David Pocock has written some excellent accounts[2]; Hsu's recent book[3] is no doubt the most incisive work written so far about the structure of division in Indian society. Sectional and communal divisions in Hindu society have been the focal theme of sociological and anthropological studies in the South Asian area for over two decades[4]. This has caused much chagrin in official quarters in India, as well as among modern Indians in India and the diaspora, who understandably frown at the study of divisions which they feel are harmful to Indian society; 'why do anthropologists insist on studying caste and division in India when there are so many more important and fascinating things happening there'—this is a representative query posed by Indian administrators and intellectuals faced with sociological conversation. Yet, regardless of the understandable feeling that these divisions ought not to exist, no amount of soft-pedalling and ever-so-well meant whitewashing can disenthuse the anthropologist in India from analysing these divisions; the sociologist *qua* sociologist is not a social therapist unless called upon to be one: but by such attempted therapy he really opts out from the less inspiring, and more modest duty of the student of society to describe society as it is and not as it should be. Caste corporate groups, and division between corporate units is not only crucial to the study and the understanding of Indian society—there is virtually no other tool available at present. Most modern Indians, however skilled in the professions, however erudite in sundry reading, do not realize the importance and the subtle dignity of purely descriptive studies; nor do they realize the important distinction between the 'is' and the 'ought'—in fact there is an endemic confusion between the two, which may well result from the unilateral, otherworldly value system of the Indian tradition which makes the 'ought' and its protagonists the cynosure of the Indian mind.

When the modern Hindu in East Africa speaks about caste, he uses the English word 'caste' even when he uses his own language, i.e., Gujarati or Panjabi. This seems to be an unconscious defence and protest device against the possible charge of being old-fashioned and socially reactionary. When talking to caste-mates, or to other Indians when matters of personal or kinship importance are discussed, they will use the names of the caste in question—Lohana, Patel, Mochi, Khattri, Ramgarhia, etc., but they will use the correct Indian term *jati* (caste) descriptively only under strong, directed pressure in their discourse. Hardly any East African Hindu feels at ease when referred to the fact that a caste (*jati*) is simply an endogamous group and that only the abolition of endogamy, or more positively, the large-scale introduction of caste exogamy would break the caste system, which they decry with much eloquence. Far apart perhaps from some of the very few learned Brahmins in East Africa, hardly anyone—not even the old, support the caste system dialectically. Yet, what they oppose, and what they suggest should be done away with, is again a figment of the 'ought'—so far as in East Africa, only few marriages have been inter-caste liaisons. The uninspiring, purely factual statement, held out by the social scientist to the East African Indian informant, that no amount of invective against the vacuous 'caste system' will help, as 'caste' is nothing but endogamy—at least in the East African setting—makes most Indians quite uncomfortable. If the point is pressed hard enough, young Indians—young not necessarily in age but in outlook, i.e., all people who would like to be identified with modern social aspirations—hasten to assure that even endogamy is breaking down, that inter-caste marriage is becoming frequent, and they would usually adduce a case from their own family or from some 'close friend' where exogamous marriages have occurred, or are about to occur. The most eloquent critics of the institution are equally aware of the insignificant number of exogamous liaisons. There is an interesting shift in the semantics of caste-parlance; sentences like 'there are many unarranged, inter-caste marriages through love' or 'there have been at least two dozens of inter-caste marriages in my community' cannot be substantiated. When it is pointed out, for instance, that between such culturally close communities of the Lohanas and Patels there have been only ten marriages in East Africa over the past fifteen years, this is admitted but then the reaction is to the effect 'but this is changing fast . . . in another thirty years, everyone will marry whom he likes'. This diction is quite universal; it also goes to show how strongly the modern Indian in East Africa has been affected by the teachings of the culture heroes of the age, Gandhi, Nehru, Bose, etc. Modern India's official culture is free of caste; that is to say, the parlance of its votaries is that of a casteless society—the only hitch being that again, 'is' language is used where 'ought' language should be used.

Just how the caste system, i.e., the tradition of *jati*-endogamous marriage is going to break down in East Africa in the near future at the present rate of inter-caste alliances, is hard to imagine, unless the political and social pressure on the minority accelerates this dormant potential of social change. It is stated, by one and all, that the 'caste system'—whatever that means to the East African Indians—has been harmful and that it must vanish. There is hardly any Indian of whatever degree of sophistication, who would argue, officially, in favour of the system. Suggestions that charity begins at home, and that the system should be broken from within the family structure, are taken in a prescriptive sense, and there is a strong tendency, on the rhetorical side, to assert that inter-caste marriages should eventually take place. However, when it comes to the parental or grandparental, or the 'arranging' generation, few of them would initiate a match across the caste-lines, even if considerable financial benefits might result; but the older, 'arranging' generations would tend to give in to the occasional entreaties of young people who want to marry across caste-lines, if such advantages are evident. Hardly any of the 'arranging' generation would admit any grudge against their descendant's partner of another caste, once the marriage had come about.

The majority of East African Indians are Gujarati-speaking Hindus; they form roughly 70 per cent of the total Asian population. Among them, the Patels and Lohanas are numerically and economically dominant—economically on a par, however, with the less numerous Shahs, most of whom are Jain by religion[5] and the *banya*, i.e., people belonging to the merchant-caste by tradition. The rest of the Gujarati Hindus belong to the '*choti jat*', literally, 'small castes', inferior to the others in the indigenous Indian caste ranking, i.e., carpenters (*sutaria*), cobblers (*muchi, mochi*), barbers (*nao*), tailors (*darji*), all of which are summarily and incorrectly referred to as the '*fundi*' class, *fundi* being the Swahili word for labourers in general, but carpenters or masons in particular. '*Fundi*' covers both Gujarati and Panjabi groups; among the latter, it is almost exclusively the Ramgarhia Sikhs who are thus referred to, as quite a few of this highly enterprising community have gone into the professions and done very well indeed. Trade exclusiveness, one of the criteria of the old, indigenous Indian caste system, has hardly ever been adhered to in East Africa, except where expert skills have been traditional, and hard to come by outside the old caste-groups; thus, the Gujarati tailors are mostly *darji* by caste, the goldsmiths are almost 100 per cent *soni*, i.e., members of the Indian Gujarati goldsmith caste. Mobility is upward unilateral, though: no 'higher' caste people do the work the *fundis* do—i.e. no or very few banyas, for instance, would take to shoe-making or tailoring, though many of the professional people among the East African Indians of this decade belong to the castes identified with the *fundi* until very recently.

Panjabi Hindus are much less divisive among themselves, and though *Khattris* (quasi-warriors or ascriptive one-time rulers), *suds*, derived from Sanskrit '*sudra*', a person of the fourth and lowest classical caste (*varna*)—of the traditional scheme, and Brahmins did not and do not intermarry in India, there is indeed a noticeable increase in intermarriages among these East African Panjabi groups, and there is much less opprobium on the side of the elders against such liaisons than there is in the Gujarati groups.

The Sikhs, very close to the Hindus or, for all sociological purposes, identifiable with the Panjabi Hindus in matters of caste-ranking and structure, are about 10 per cent *Jat*, i.e., members of the Panjabi indigenous agricultural and petty-landowning caste, and 90 per cent Ramgarhias, which caste was ranked close to the bottom of the traditional ranking in the Panjab. As indicated above, they form the bulk of the actual *fundi*, i.e., the acting masons, carpenters, etc. They are definitely the most successful and excellent artisans in East Africa, a fact admitted both by the indigenous Africans and the European settlers.

There is a small group of Panjabi Muslims of the *Sunni* tradition and of the recently founded Ahmeddiya or Mirza'i sect, diffusely present in the East African countries, most of them in government and other clerical services. There is free social intercourse between them and the other Panjabi speakers, as socializing is language-rather than caste-bound in East Africa.

Whether the Goans can be classified as Indian in East Africa is a ticklish question for anyone except the anthropologist. For the latter, it is perfectly clear that the Goans are Indians, whether they want to be thus identified or not. They speak an Indian language

(Konkani, very close to Marathi), and there is no other justifiable classification from any ethnical or cultural viewpoint. Most Goans in East Africa, however, are not too happy with this designation, and they would stress their 'Portuguese-style' Catholicism as a point of cultural difference. The few Goans in the professions, doctors and lawyers, are either radically Indian by a sheer effort of will, or they deny or ignore their Indian background—I have met a few who go as far as to claim that they are Portuguese or Brazilian! But even they have quite a hard time in convincing people that they do not understand Hindustani, the lingua franca of East African Indians. The phenomenon, incidentally, of 'not knowing', i.e., pretending not to understand a language identification with other speakers, is one of the more noxious experiences of the sociological profession. Whether this is due to the prolonged non-acceptance of such a group by the host nation or by the mother-group, the case of the Goan psychiatrist who claims to be Brazilian is no less aggravating than that of the German-born Jew in Chicago who moved to Pittsburgh for a while in order to be able to tell people he was from Pittsburgh when they asked him where he came from. Many Goans under forty, however, do not speak Konkani even, having had a 'purely English' education.

The three Gujarati-speaking Muslim groups form a very important sector of the Indian minority. Among them, the Shi'a Khoja Ishmailis, the followers of H.H. the Aga Khan, are from any viewpoint the most conspicuously emancipated, and perhaps the most successful group among all the sections of the minority, beginning with their apparel: their women wear western dress due to a *firman* (pontifical injunction) of the late Aga Khan. They are the most thoroughly modernized—at least on the outside—but certainly also the most alienated from among the Indian groups, tending to keep aloof from the others. Moreover, they have succeeded in creating a separate identity in the alter-image of all other people in East Africa.

The next largest Gujarati Muslim group are the Shia'a Khoja Ithna-Asharis, followers of the eleventh Imam. The *mullahs* of this community are frequently North Indians or Panjabis by birth, probably because there is more Arabic, and certainly more Urdu learning in those Indian and Pakistani regions.

The third and last Gujarati Muslim group are the Bohras or Boros. Whereas both the Ishmailis and the Ithna-Asharis are Lohana by descent, converted to Shi'ism at different points in the past, the Bohras are of Gujarati Brahmin background. The head of this sect, who bears the illustrious title '*Dai-ul-mutlaq*' ('emissary of communion', i.e., with the hidden Imam, the representative of the Prophet), sits in Bombay.

The denial of caste in the Islamic groups in India, Pakistan and Indian East Africa is a purely theoretical and pietistic claim. Endogamy within the various Islamic groups mentioned is as rigid as among the Hindus. There have been virtually no intermarriages between Ithna-Asharis, Ishmailis and Bohras, nor between any of the three Gujarati and the two Panjabi Muslim groups. I cannot help feeling that there is less latent opposition against possible marriages with non-Indians, whites that is, among the Ishmailis, than against liaisons with other-group Muslims. Such liaisons, which are not quite rare especially with Ishmailis who studied in Britain or elsewhere abroad and contracted their own match, are less frowned upon than marriages across religious, caste and linguistic lines inside the Indian minority. This may simply be due to the 'one-is-less-than-two-harms-done' count: in an Indian-non-Indian liaison, only one Indian family is hurt in prestige and emotion, in the case of inter-community marriages within the Indian groups, two Indian families are.

Whereas the divisions between the five Muslim sections (three Gujarati and two Panjabi) are pretty clear, this cannot be said about all the Hindu Gujarati communities. There is a general identification of all Gujaratis except the Muslims as 'Hindus'; both Lohanas and Patels, when using the word 'Hindu', without previous contemplation, mean Gujarati-or-Cutchi-speaking Hindus only (Cutchi is a western dialect of Gujarati). The term 'Cutchi' is used by most non-Gujaratis and for all Gujaratis in East Africa, and often by Africans for all Indians. Gujaratis do not semantically include Panjabis as 'Hindus' unless the fact that many Panjabis in East Africa are Hindu is directly pointed out to them; yet such cognitive knowledge does not in any way decrease the divisive tendency—one does not mix or marry with another group just because they are Hindu, but because they belong to the same linguistic and endogamous unit. Just as in contemporary India, there is really no conflict between the '*choti jat*' 'small (low) castes' like the *sutarias* and *muchis*, and the dominant Lohana-Patel groups, because their respective ranking is so heterogenous that social, let alone matrimonial competition and eligibility does not really arise. On the other hand—again like in India—there is a strongly divisive, potentially hostile undercurrent between Patels and Lohanas, the culturally and caste-hierarchically closest communities. In the first place, the mutual alter-image between them is largely negative; Patel informants tend to call the Lohanas shrewd, the Lohana women flippant or unhappy, prone to despair and suicide; Lohana informants would say about the same with regard to the Patels. Yet there is a strong readiness on principle to intermarry, and about a dozen Lohana-Patel intermarriages have taken place recently in East Africa. The fact that in these matches the men were Patel, the women Lohana, might be a case of hypergamy—the Hindu male can marry slightly below his caste-level without any orthodox opposition; and this is also a corroboration of the fact that in India, the Patels have a slightly higher caste-ranking than the Lohanas, where they live in the same or immediately adjacent areas.

The former Indian custom of non-commensality between the castes has vanished in East Africa. All castes interdine, and a significant proportion of non-commensality may be present only between the linguistically different groups. This, however, may also be due to the very different kind of food Gujaratis and Panjabis prepare—and there is little common taste in culinary matters. Very few Gujaratis are seen at the average Panjabi wedding and *vice versa*. Menfolk drink together, and there is real and total integration of every group in East Africa, indigenous, Asian, and European, on the sundowner (equivalent of the American cocktail) level. There is also an unwritten bond between meat-eaters and alcohol-drinkers, probably the strongest commensal bond across the caste- and language-lines in the minority. 'Advanced' often means just meat-eating and whisky-consuming. Within the upper Gujarati communities, there is latent conflict but not so much among the Lohanas as among the Patels. At Nairobi and some other larger settlements, there is the 'Patel Brotherhood' and the 'Patel Club', the former being the ascriptively vegetarian and tee-totalling, the latter the 'indulging' section—always referring to the males, as very few women as yet 'indulge'. Tension between the Lohanas and the Patels seems to transcend earthly life—as in some places the Lohanas and the Patels have separate cremation grounds.

Among the Patels, there are two further endogamous units, the *Kharwas* and the *Lewas*, whose original locations are geographically distant in the Gujarat. This restriction to intra-caste endogamy is kept up by and large, conscious only to the older people who know about it, but who do not communicate it to the younger generation in the process of finding mates. Thus, though young couples in arranged marriages do not usually know about the intra-endogamous background of their match, the separation between the two groups persists in East Africa; a large proportion of the Patels in East Africa are *Lewa*.

Brahmins are few and far between in East Africa. Among the Gujaratis, there are about 300 families in all East Africa, mostly of the *Audich*-section; their socio-religious organization is the Brahma Samaj in the main cities; among Panjabis, there are roughly one hundred Brahmin houses in all the territories. Brahmins find it easier to steer clear of communal divisions, for although no particular ritualistic status attaches to them, they are welcome as guests in all groups.

Communal divisions in this context are a purely anthropological matter; the casual observer, particularly when he listens to the conversation of the modernized Hindus who make strenuous efforts to give the impression that there is no such thing as communal division, is easily persuaded that they either no longer exist or that they do not pose a social problem any more; or that, where they exist, they are vestigial and about to vanish within the next few years. The rather embarrassing vociferousness and the vehement denial of division on *jati*-lines is quite clearly a device of overcompensation; unconscious to most of the younger people, it has possibly a cathartic effect on the speaker, against his better cognitive knowledge of the divisive situation.

Division on communal bases had a positive side also: it was the parochial groups alone that have so far created educational, medical and other crucial facilities, where an all-over appeal to the Asians, say, through the Indian Association, was never made or failed. This and similar non-parochial Asian societies are diffusely present; their function is somewhat theoretical—exhausting itself in the reception of international and Indian guests, and in giving status to their appointed leaders and in similar marginal offices. The organizations which build and sustain schools, hospitals, assembly halls, libraries, etc., are parochial without exception. On the practical side, the various communities, deeply suspicious of each other, readily admit each other's achievements, and compete in a healthy way. There is hardly any Lohana, Patel or other Hindu, who would seriously impugn the excellence of the Khoja Ishmaili achievements by way of creating and sustaining social work, education, etc. on a large scale, and *vice versa*. Thus all groups admit that the Aga Khan hospitals and schools are the best in the countries, closely followed by those of the Jain Shahs, and then perhaps by the Arya Samaj which is largely Panjabi.

Parochially founded and supported educational institutions today are nominally interracial in their teaching staff and in the recruitment of students. Even previous to governmental injunctions after *uhuru* outlawing discrimination on racial or communal grounds, there was always a tendency to include some students of different racial and religious origin, although the founding group would be dominant both on the staff and in the student body. The Aga Khan hospitals in Nairobi and Dar es Salaam have approximately an equal number of Ishmaili and other patients, though there is a preponderance of Ishmaili doctors and nurses on their staff. This, of course, is very largely due to the superior encouragement toward higher education and training in the Ishmaili community in general, as pioneers of western-oriented emancipation among the Asian minority.

All agree, in their small talk and in common parlance at least, that communal divisions must go and the younger and more radical people claim that they are gone, which of course is a sample of the aforesaid systematic confusion of 'is' and 'ought' endemic in Indian society. A rather interesting linguistic use is made, after *uhuru*, of communal division on its most basic, i.e. endogamous level. The African and European allegation that 'Asians don't mix', meaning that they do not intermarry and that they do not *really* socialize with others, is often countered by stating that they do not intermarry at all, and socialize very little, with Indians of other castes and linguistic groups and of different religion—and that the relative seclusion of the Asian minority as a whole from non-Asians should be appreciated as an *a fortiori*.

When outsiders are present, the urgency of mutual assimilation is so strong that statements of the form 'the Patels (non-Patels speaking) . . . do (something negative or pejorative)' or 'the Khoja Ishmailis are . . . . (pejorative)' are becoming very rare indeed. Mutual generalizing criticism is thus becoming a strictly intra-Indian affair.

The question is constantly being asked if and how Indians should integrate in the new African body politic; whatever may be the views about it, and they vary quite radically from person to person, the variance not being bound up with specific groups, there is always the stipulation that the Indians would first have to integrate themselves i.e. abandon caste and linguistic divisions, before the next step can be taken.

'Sundowner' level socialization serves as a figurative paradigm for integration; just how seriously it is taken by non-Asians is not a speculation within the purview of this chapter. It is true, however, that inter-group and interracial reservations are completely relaxed where Asian men, and much fewer women, between themselves and with non-Asians, drink together. But the very fact that drinking, on which there is still a strong stigma, is a positive leaven for integration, makes the word 'integration' suspect to the more conservative Indians.

Social intercourse in young peer groups, schools, scout organizations, sports clubs, etc., is complete and uninhibited. On the adult level, the B.S.S., the East African corollary of the Hindu Fascist R.S.S. (*Rashtriya Svayam Sevak Sangh*, National Self Help Organization) has Gujarati and Panjabi speakers of all castes in its fold, male only, as female companionship is thought dangerous and disruptive on the orthodox compeer level. Here the ease of social relations is forced, but there is total integration, except that Muslims would not join for obvious reasons.

As said at the beginning, prediction is none of the anthropologist's job—all divisive tendencies may indeed break down in the not too distant future. Asians find it hard to appreciate the social scientist's refusal to prophesy, and his reluctance to state and to see unity which may well come about some day, but which just is not yet there.

Statements to the effect that religion ranks supreme in the Indian value systems are by now sheer platitudes; yet the statement that this feature extends to the Indian settlers in East Africa is important and has to be made quite categorically. Just as no secular value system has ever developed in India from indigenous roots, East African Indians have been arranging all their values on a non-secular scale, again with the ascetic as the cynosure in that scale. We must rule out the objections that come from all sides, that 'money' is the only value for the Asians in East Africa, as a facile and dilettante view of no use to the social scientist. For even the love of money ties in with the unilateral hierarchical, teleologically religious core-value of the Asians in this region.

Like in India, the older Indian in East Africa tends to be taken in by the itinerant monk *sahdu*, *pandit*, story-teller, diviner and faith-healer who gets to East Africa from India as an invitee or on his own, even though most Hindus always assert that these people are rogues and no good, and that they should not be supported. The reception and the attitude toward 'saints' and other preachers of institutionalized 'big tradition' Hinduism is still more naive, and bespeaks a higher degree of floating credulousness than in the present day sister communities in India.

What kind of religion is it that the preachers from India disseminate and reiterate on their extended, usually quite lucrative East African trips? And what is the religion the Asians brought along with them? How has it been modified through the decades of Indian residence in East Africa? Here, the 'big tradition—little tradition' dichotomy will aid our analysis.[6] Officially, there is no 'little tradition' in East Africa. Hindu religious organizations have usurped the total capacity of official religious communication, and even the more esoteric among these societies (the Swaminarayan sect, the followers of Sai Baba, a.o.) identify themselves completely with the standards of the 'big tradition', i.e. the Vedas and Upanishads, the Bhagavadgita, and the didactic epic. The demographic cause for this is simply that there are hardly any rural settlers in the true sense; even the petty *duka* owner (shopkeeper) in the bush is not a villager among African villagers or herdsmen, but a permanent guest from the city, as it were, and too isolated culturally to establish a rapprochement with the African 'little traditions' that no doubt surround him. A homogeneous cultural group has to settle in a locality for quite a while in order to develop original 'little tradition' tendencies of its own, and, for example, the rough and hardy Sikhs who trade hides with the people in Masailand and who live very much like their clients, hardly have the opportunity to develop 'little traditions' first because their womenfolk seldom live with them in the bush (and 'little traditions' do not develop where there are no women of the same culture group around), secondly because the minimal Sikh prayers are so short and handy that the Sikh trader in Masailand will hardly feel the necessity for any superogatory religious activity.

First, then, the 'big tradition' proper among the East African Indians. The Muslims' religious life is easy to describe. Most of the East African Indian Muslims are Shia'a, professing an eclectic Islam with emphasis on a linear continuity in the transmission of the teachings through successors or successor-surrogates to the Prophet. Thus, the Panjabi Ahmeddiyas or Mirzai's ascribe a status identical with that of the Prophet to their founder in the nineteenth century. Similar in structure, but very different in temperament and style, the Ishmailis regard the living Aga Khan as the *hazir Imam* 'the present Imam—Leader of the Faith' ('present' in the sense of 'living', 'physically present'), and they claim linear descent from the Prophet's own line for him. To the Ithna-Asharis, though they do not believe in a contemporary accessible Imam, the continuity of the prophetic office is taken care of by anyone who is directly inspired by the voice of God, so that any votary who is pious and has some charismatic status is eligible. The influence of the Hindu *avataravada* (divinity reincarnated in human teachers according to the spiritual needs of the time), to which Islam had been exposed for so many centuries and by which it had been thoroughly modified in South Asia, is strikingly evident in these forms of Islamic religion. The Bohras, Gujarati speakers of Brahmin descent, believe in a Hidden Imam, represented by the *Dai-ul-mutlaq* mentioned earlier in another context. There has hardly been any change in the practice of Islamic religion since the departure from India. There is a considerable amount of successful conversion among Africans, especially through the Ahmeddiyas, who are most energetic proselytizers and whose preachers 'go native' in a radical way; they master the African languages to a degree that enables them to preach in Swahili, Kikuyu, and other East African languages.

This does not hold for the Khoja Ishmailis, for their religious outlook has changed most radically since the time their ascendants came to East Africa. Whether the purely historical accident that the late Aga Khan, a modern intellectual, a humanist and a cosmopolitan issued *firmans* (canonical injunctions) which modernized the community by decree, or whether there is an inherent lenience in the Ishmaili version of Muslim teachings, or if they both combined to change the community, is hard to assess. Ishmaili Islam is the most highly personalized form; based on the ascriptive charisma of the Aga Khan's person, the highly reformist, sophisticated, and pragmatically extremely functional notions of the late Aga Khan have changed the face of this important, affluent and striking group. The late and the present young Aga Khan, a graduate from Harvard University, have been sending their *firmans* by letter or wire, and they are then read out from the pulpit, in the *Jamatkhana* (assembly halls—the Ishmaili name for their mosque and place of congregation) and these orders take effect immediately. Some of these *firmans* are of a strictly mundane nature, as for instance that the cost of a bride's gown should not exceed 30 shillings and that the number of wedding guests should be limited to a specific figure—the change-over to western dress has already been mentioned.

The Hindus and other non-Islamic groups among the Indians admit and admire the Aga Khan's leadership and regret that

Hinduism has not brought forth a similar personality, or a similar pattern of incontrovertible, personal leadership.

With the exception of the Ishmailis, the official worship and ritual is identical among the other Islamic groups. They are supposed to say their formalistic prayers (*namaz*) four or five times a day, and it seems the Ahmeddiyas and Ithna-Asharis are modally the most regular. The Ishmailis have a special prayer book, culled from the Quran, but with certain modifications; they now pray again in Arabic, formerly in Gujarati. They stress meditation— the *Jamatkhanas* in the East African cities are indeed fairly full from 4.30 every morning, and a large majority attend the obligatory Friday prayers and conventions. The *Jamatkhanas*, some of them architecturally extremely modernistic, are not only places for prayer, but for a highly institutionalized type of community life; food is prepared in Ishmaili homes, brought to the *Jamatkhana*, and auctioned, so that people who do not cook (bachelors, or very poor people in all sorts of duress) can have a well cooked meal almost at any time—the proceeds of this food auction go to the poor-fund, and this feeds back into the various social and educational institutions of the Aga Khan.

The alter-image of the Ishmailis in the eyes of other Indian communities, however, is not too positive. In the first place, most Indians distinguish between 'Muslims' and 'Ishmailis', including the Ishmailis themselves. When asked, 'is Mr. X an Ishmaili?' most Indians will answer 'no, he is a Muslim': and if you ask an Ishmaili 'are you a Muslim?', he is likely to say, 'no, I am an Ishmaili'. In the eyes of the other Muslim groups, the Ishmaili ritual, prayer, and the general development of religion is heretical, too much re-moved from the orthodox conventions of worship. Though none of the Shi'a sects in East Africa would concur with the puristic post-ulates of the *ulema* (the official body of orthodox Islam), censure of the Ishmaili form of worship is about as strong as that of non-Muslim worship in general. There is a strong tendency among other Muslims and Hindus in East Africa to suspect Ishmailis in general of moral laxity, and in accordance with the official Indian culture 'immorality' etc. means any autonomous expression of the sexual. However, the only clue the non-Ishmailis can possibly have is that Ishmaili women wear frocks—baring one's legs as a female being is a *chose fatale* to the Indian mind even in 1965. Objectively, there is no modal difference in the 'moral habits' of the Ishmailis from any other Indian community, Muslim, Hindu, or other. Somehow, the image of an Indian woman not covering her ankles engenders suspicion. Interviewing Ishmailis of all economic groups, and of all relevant age-groups, it was found that their attitudes about morality, sex, and the invariable value concomitance of sex and morality is identical with that of all other groups, with not the slightest difference in the mode of appraisal and censure.

Hindu influence, contextually and formally, is strong on all Indian Muslims. Hardly any Indian Islam is *'ulema* Islam, and certainly no East African Indian Islam bears any trace of the *'ulema* strictures. But although both Shi'ism and Sunism tended to incorporate many Hindu elements on South Asian soil, including the virtual acceptance of *avataras* or divine teachers in human form, incarnations or emanations of the godhead, it seems to this author that the East African Indian Muslims have absorbed more Hindu elements than they are conscious of. Hindu symbolism abounds in Ishmaili nomenclature—I saw a house in Dar es Salaam named *Om Habibabad*. When I questioned some Ishmailis around the house if they knew the meaning of OM (which is the basic Hindu-Brahmin vocal symbol, and as a written symbol comparable in importance to the cross of the Christians), they said it was some sort of a Persian or Arabic *'mantra'* (a *mantra* again is a secret, sacred Hindu or Buddhist formula). Of course, there is nothing whatever Muslim about OM, but the cathexis is all the stronger as its original content has been forgotten.

Hinduism in East Africa, like elsewhere, is in every aspect far more complex than Islam. Like in India, there is no such thing as a church or a pervasive ecclesiastic organization among the Hindus. The only well-organized Hindu group, at least in matters of uniform ritual and credo, is the *Arya Samaj*, a highly fundamentalistic, simplistic, and theologically unsophisticated reform sect founded by Swami Daynanda Sarasvati, a Gujarati monk, who taught mainly in the Panjab in the middle of the last century. It has caught the imagination of many East African Indians—among whom the large majority are Panjabi with a small Gujarati element —perhaps due to the feeling of a lack of unity among the Hindus of East Africa. The founder of the *Arya Samaj* ('Society of Aryans') preached 'back to the Veda', by which he meant a complete ritualistic identification and adherence to the oldest portion of the canonical scripture, the *samhita*—collections of hymns; he excluded the Upanishads and the other speculative tracts of the Vedic tradition, which set him into crass contrast with all other Hindu sects. In Northern India, especially again in the Panjab, the unreformed, allegedly more conservative Hindus refer to themselves as '*Sanatani*' (eternal). The *Sanatan Dharma Sabha* ('Organization of the Followers of the Eternal Religion') is contrasted with the *Arya Samaj*. Although the *Sanatani* are opposed to the *Arya Samaj* by their allegedly more rigid traditionalism and orthodoxy, this distinction does not stand any critical scrutiny. The *Arya Samaj* is much more fundamentalistic, and doctrinarily much less tolerant than the *Sanatana* organization. The followers of the *sanatana* tradition—and this means in East Africa, every Hindu who is not an *Arya Samajist*— use icons (*murti*) for their worship, and the main point of criticism the *Arya Samaj* teachers bring against the *sanatana* doctrines and practices centres on the latters' worship of idols. But neither the *Arya Samajists* nor the *Sanatanists* in East Africa are aware of the traditional implications of *murtipuja* (idol-worship), which has never been the worship of an inanimate object, but the aesthetical contemplation of an object in order to facilitate the contemplation of the divine in the devotee. Apart from some very few Brahmin priests (*purohit*) in East Africa which defend *murtipuja* on a scholastic level, the *Sanatanis* usually are diffident when faced by *Arya Samajist* argument, and half-heartedly admit the shortcomings of *murtipuja*.

Among the followers of the *Arya Samaj*, which is organized on an all-East African level with its administrative centre in Nairobi, the official iconoclasm of this school does not affect most of its members to the extent that all of them forswear *murtipuja* completely; most women in *Arya Samaj* households carry on with worship of Hindu gods, and of Hindu icons in their homes; men, even when staunch Samajists, usually do not interfere. From about one hundred *Samaji* households which I visited, only six insisted on not having any residual *murtipuja* in their houses; they conduct the daily Vedic fire-ritual (*havan*) in the simplified and plain version prescribed by Swami Dayananda, and the women participate in it. In all the other cases, the women live their own parallel religious life; they worship through their *murtis* (icons) although perhaps not with the same eclat as the official *Sanatanis*. As a justification of the presence of icons in the house, the *Arya Samajist* may say that he too worships Rama, Krishna, etc. as teachers; but they deny the concept of *avataras*, i.e. of divine incarnation in the forms of these mythological figures. Most *Samajists* chant the Vedic hymns without understanding their meaning, and the quality of the chant is poor; there is hardly any guidance as to correct incantation, etc.; also, the participation of women in the fire-ritual (*havan*) is totally unacceptable to the more learned, orthodox Hindus in India; Swami Dayananda's insistence on ritualistic equality of women stemmed from his desire to emancipate them socially. But this regular ritual makes the *Arya Samajist* more conservative than the Sanatanis, who are 'the conservatives' by definition. The pouring of *ghee* (clarified butter) into the sacrificial fire during the *havan* is explained by followers who want to be 'modern and scientific' as having the purpose of purifying the air in the house! The *Sanatanis* do not have a unified, organized form of ritual, every active *Sanatani* very largely concocts his private ritual, largely on information obtained from some casual teachers or itinerant preachers from India, or by emulation and counsel from his elders or peers. The *Arya Samaj* is a model for the 'big tradition'. But as all the other Hindu groups have recently been exposed to highly sophisticated forms of Hindu thought, through literature and through the visiting swamis, the travelling salesmen of the Hindu Renaissance, the 'big tradition' pervades the whole community in an overt fashion, and we shall have to look elsewhere for manifestations of the 'little tradition'; to these we must now proceed.

There are situations where some 'little tradition' surreptitiously encroaches upon 'big tradition' in East Africa, in a manner which has no exact parallel in India, simply because there is hardly any physical contiguity between the two types of tradition in such a direct manner in India. The Indians of East Africa are urban people, whatever their ancestral background. In Indian cities, the 'little traditions', where they exist sporadically, are completely subservient to the 'big traditions' and the urban followers of 'big tradition' Hinduism look down upon 'little traditions' or deny their existence altogether. Not so in East Africa. I have heard no less than a dozen reports about occurrences in different locations in all the three countries; I observed three which I regard sufficiently typical. The one case was in Tabora, Tanganyika, where 'God has come into the house' ('*ghar men Isvar aya*') of a man who claims to have daily visions of the god, Lord Krishna in his case, in person. A large number of people gather at his house which has now achieved the nimbus of a shrine and which is also marked by a flag like official temples. These visitors, by no means all women, come to witness the daily scene and very few people in the city, apart from *Arya Samajists*, would radically deny the 'truth' of these events. There is a tendency among 'modern' people to dismiss these things as *andhavisvas* (blind faith, superstition), but that is about the maximal criticism offered. Men, when together, tend to call it all fraud (*dhoka*) thus giving a seal to their scepticism which is thought to be a sign of being modern. Every morning, then, the said person feeds milk to the 'photo' of Krishna, one of the usual rather ghastly polychromes that abound in non-institutionalized places of worship all over East Africa and India, by putting a *lotha* (conic brass vessel) of sweetened milk to the lips of the painting. I moved quite close up to the image, as the householder had invited me to visit his shrine set up in a niche in his home, lately enclosed by a wooden partition which he had erected after the deity had started giving his '*darshan*' (vision, sight). The milk, as expected, oozed down to the ground on the front side of the image, which natural fact was pointed out by some of the more sceptical folks in the neighbourhood. Most of the devotees at the place actually believe that the milk is physically taken and drunk by the god, thus accepting the offer every day, thereby blessing the householder. People who deny it, pointing out the fact that the milk pours down the front as it would from any other vertical surface, are called '*nastik*' (unbelievers) by the others, and this is a term of grave religious reproach.

Most of the 'little tradition' incidences, however, fall within the wide scope of 'possession' as used by the ethnographer and the culture-and-personality oriented psychologist. The orthodox term (Gujarati and Hindustani in East Africa) is *mata* (or *devata*) *lag gayi*', literally 'the Mother (or any other deity) has affixed herself (i.e. on the person affected)'. In most cases, the Universal Mother (*Jagadamba*), or some other mother-deity, is the focus of mythological introjection; *Jagadamba* is the most frequent Gujarati appellation for the 'big tradition' mother goddess otherwise called Durga, Kali, Shakti, etc., in other parts of India. But though the goddess is of 'big tradition' provenance, her uses here are 'little tradition' uses; and of course, it is never quite certain whether a deity with a Sanskritic, i.e., 'big tradition' name, is not a Sanskritization of some local village deity, absorbed into the official pantheon. The frequent identification of '*Mata*' (mother) with Shitla, the goddess of smallpox, would be a pointer in that direction.

In most cases in East Africa, this sort of possession is accompanied by the ascribed capacity of divination, soothsaying and healing. I studied a man in his early fifties in Old Kampala (Uganda), who has since hoisted a tall pole with a red flag—red being the emblematic colour of the mother goddess —and a *trishul*, the trident symbolizing both the 'Mother' and her divine spouse, Shiva.

Regularly every Sunday at 9 p.m., he invokes the blessings of the 'Mother', begins to tremble and shake vehemently within a few minutes after his invocations, which are in Gujarati. After that, he calms down completely and for the rest of the performance he acts and talks perfectly normally as it would seem. He distributes holy ash and *prasad* (sweets offered to the deity) to the rapt audience, which numbers between 10 and 50 every week. He then answers queries about the future and solves problems of anyone who asks him any specific personal questions. A British-educated, delight-fully charming and attractive Lohana girl of about 20 told me 'I believe him completely, because he is really in close contact with the Universal Mother whom I also worship'—interestingly, the young lady's father is a staunch and active *Arya Samajist*—but his wife and daughters are not disenthused by this austere fact: the bell tolls at almost every hour of the day in the little house temple which the women in the family run in dire opposition to the *Arya Samajist* injunctions against idols. However, when I asked the young lady whether the divinations of the man possessed had always come true, she first answered in the affirmative; after some reflection she added 'but once, when I wanted something very very badly, he promised me I would get it. But then it did not come through! When later on I asked him to justify this false outcome, the holy man said that what God gives you, my little daughter, is always the best for you'.

The most interesting case which I studied personally was that of a Lohana woman of about 40 at Mwanza, Tanganyika, whose house has been visited in a somewhat bizarre fashion by the Universal Mother. It is a very ordinary house. A while ago children heard strange songs and footsteps one night and when they opened the door to the little shrine in the morning, there were cinnabar powder footprints of a small female foot, though without the big toe, on the floor in front of the idol; by its side, there was a crude *trishul* (trident sacred to Shiva and the Universal Mother), also of *kunkum* (cinnabar powder). This, so the woman and her devotees reported, was repeated several times, and subsequently, the footprint and the *trishul* were covered by the woman with a piece of glass, in order to preserve the holy token. Sizable numbers of women and some men have been visiting the place every day since, and the matter got into the *East African Standard* and the *Nation*, the two most widely read English language dailies in East Africa —as did some similar events at sporadic intervals. A Gujarati lady doctor, an M.B.B.S. from Bombay, herself suggested to me to witness the scene because she had felt perturbed by the scepticism which I had pronounced in a talk to the local Hindu community, criticizing the whole syndrome from a pastoral view point. The lady doctor, whose age is about 35, is herself a staunch believer in the powers of the woman and she introduced the latter to me in person. I am personally almost certain the woman is a latent catatonic-schizophrenic with a strong paranoid tendency. She functions normally enough in her home, looking after nine children of her own, and her husband. She talks gently, though nervously and apologetically when objective questions are put to her. She is not illiterate. Every morning she takes her bath, then proceeds to her shrine. She invokes the goddess with a short, obviously self-composed Gujarati prayer, which she says with hands upraised, and which hardly lasts five minutes. In course of this, and for about ten minutes after she has concluded her prayer, she trembles vehemently, her eyes are closed and she perspires profusely; yet, it did not strike me as an unpleasant sight. Now when she emerges, her hands are frequently full of *kunkum* (cinnabar powder), and this is the most awe-inspiring feat in the eyes of the pious public. It is hinted that the *kunkum* is somehow mysteriously put into her hands by the goddess herself. Some of the ladies told me that at several occasions, the whole little shrine was full of *kunkum*, walls, floor, ceiling, and everything, after she had completed her prayers. I inspected her hands, and there were indeed slight cinnabar powder traces between her palms. It seems that the moment she enters her shrine, she touches the little altar, or the space between the image of the deity and a little wooden partition around it. The image is one of the common gaudy oleographs, probably torn from a calendar, and it is not even framed in glass. Below the actual 'photo' of the goddess, who sits astride the tiger, the *vahana* (carrier animal of the goddess Durga or Shakti) there is a thick layer of *kunkum*, broad at the base, and tapering off at the spot of the paper where the goddess' feet are painted. This *kunkum* was supposed to originate *in loco*, and when it wears away as it does, the goddess replenishes it at night. Little bits of *kunkum* thus probably come into contact with the protrusions of the woman's palms as she touches the area; she then rubs her palms vigorously, which movement is interpreted as a gesture of prayer by the devotees; but this process obviously spreads the powder all over her palms. If this is the actual procedure, it is probably quite unconscious, because the woman evidently forgets, or does not absorb these preparations as her own—which is quite typical for several types of schizophrenia. The people who are really upset about these recurrent and prestige-giving events are the *Arya Samajists*, who refer to all of them, and especially to the reaction of the audience, as *andha-visvas*, which is a literal translation-neologism from English meaning 'blind faith', but which Asian English speakers re-interpret as 'superstition'. They also imply that these matters involve deliberate fraudulence; in the case of the Mwanza woman, however, I am perfectly certain that there is no such thing as deliberate make-believe; it is one of the pathological manifestations of 'little tradition' Hinduism for which the majority of all Hindus has always found some place.

A young man in Nairobi, about 32, Panjabi *khattri*, clerk in a bank, who speaks perfectly good English, is married, and has two children, has been having '*darshan*' (vision, consummative 'sight' of the chosen deity) and other 'spiritual experiences' of Shiva and Shakti, the consort of Shiva, a synonym of *Jagadamba*, the Universal Mother, ever since he was a boy of three, so he told me. A *trishul* (trident symbol of Shiva and Shakti), has been appearing in blood on his forehead, on his arms and chest, and so did the mystic syllable OM in Nagari script. About ten years ago, so he told me, he found a *guru* in Nairobi, strangely enough an old Sikh of the Ramgarhia caste, who taught him 'how to meditate and see God correctly'. Helped by his *guru*, and aided by his own previous experiences, he had been in states of 'profound meditation', in which he sees brilliant lights, and the full vision of the god and the goddess, sometimes together, sometimes separately. Once, a few years ago, he further told me—as he had told his friends and relatives—he was in deep *samadhi* (consummative trance, the final postulate of the Hindu's contemplative exercise) for three days on end. Though he sat in his room at home all the time, a person who was his exact double did all his work in the office, signed papers for him with precisely his handwriting, and when he returned to the office on the fourth day, nobody had noticed his absence. He also met a man of the *darji* (Gujarati tailor) caste from Arusha, Tanganyika, who was an expert in '*maili vidya*' ('dirty' techniques, viz. sorcery)—as was, incidentally, the brother of his own *guru*, who changed into a big bird and began sucking his (the speaker's) blood.

This is a pathological, but not infrequent example of little-big tradition transaction: the experiences themselves are very much of the 'little tradition', but the jargon is entirely that of the Hindu Renaissance 'big tradition' of modern India, the style, without modification, that of Vivekananda, Shivananda, and copious other dificatory literature of the contemporary Hindu revival.

These are not just isolated cases; on a cautious estimate, there must be around two to three hundred instances, currently, of the pathological-cum-'little' tradition framework in East Africa. Adducing some examples in detail as we did was not to accumulate empirical data for corroboration; what is important for our study is not so much the number of occurrences, as the size of the audience to these phenomena: this is a problem well known to the student of culture and personality, viz. the definition of the mentally 'normal' and 'abnormal' in terms of acceptance, neglect, or rejection by the environmental society. We are not so much concerned, therefore, with showing a great number of pathological cases, accepted with positive evaluation in a specific religious tradition in a transplanted milieu, but with the exemplification of an interesting syndrome important for cultural analysis: the terms 'normal' and 'abnormal' in a clinical sense are completely vacuous, if they are not used within a specific audience *vis-a-vis* the agents or performers for this audience. Most of the cases that can be adduced to exemplify a 'little tradition' overlap with Hindu 'big tradition' in East Africa, which goes to show that the most bizarre behaviour pattern can and does gain prestige if there is a sanctioning audience. But again, the psychological accoutrements of this situation are of no real concern to us in this study; what is important is to realize that the Hindu settlers in East Africa have achieved a complete fusion of 'big' and 'little' tradition elements, albeit at the cost of both theological and psychological congruity.

Unlike in South Africa[7], the gods and goddesses by which the Hindu subjects in East Africa are affected or possessed, are exclusively 'big tradition' deities. The Gujaratis and Panjabis who migrated to East Africa did not have any godlings comparable to, say, the Seven Sisters of the Dravidian rural pantheon. They came with a predominantly urban background, and with urban, i.e., mercantile purposes. Whatever 'little tradition' had encroached upon the settlers' parents or grandparents from the rural areas of the Gujarat or the Panjab had been crowded out by 'big tradition' parlance and its postulates, so that it requires a considerable amount of probing to find 'little tradition' residues except on the pathological fringe. Most of the 'big tradition—little tradition' overlap goes on inside the Hindu households in East Africa, special fasts (*brat*), the daily *puja* (formal worship at the house shrine), are carried out largely by the women. These are oriented towards the Sanskritic gods, i.e. the deities of the Hindu 'big trad tion', in Gujarati and in Panjabi, with a sprinkling of Sanskn invocations among the former, and of course the Sanskrit stereotyp formulae of the *Arya Samajis*.

There is a very large Gujarati sect which might be said to represe an Essenic form of crystallized 'big tradition' Hinduism. It is th Swaminarayan cult created about a hundred years ago by a high ascetical Brahmin and his followers in the Gujarat. Their di ciplinary and doctrinary canon is the *patrika* (literally, 'letter'), a set rigid rules of ritualistic and personal behaviour. This sect has larg and well-kept temples in almost all East African cities, and in son places (as in Tororo, Uganda) their shrine is larger and mo elaborate than the other, more general Hindu temples. Th Swaminarayanis are also more exclusive than other Hindu group although they do not object to other people entering and worshippir at their temples, their services are more uniform, more formalize and more intensive than most of the other Hindu forms of worshi They are also highly selective about visiting preachers; they invi only preachers from the mother-body in the Gujarat, specialis in the teachings of the sect. Their present swami, who is 'th same as Narayana (God, Vishnu)' visited the region; when he spok a screen had to be put up to conceal the female audience from h vision; the homes in which he stayed had to be evacuated by a women of the household between menarche and menopaus Their doctrines, however, do not seem to be different in essenc from those of the orthodox Hindus around them; they worshi Vishnu and his various human incarnations (Rama, Krishna), a well as Shiva, the Devi, and the other main deities of the Hind pantheon, images of whom are installed in the Swaminaraya temples side by side with 'photos' of the three monastic founde Brahmins. These original teachers, however, are seen as suprem in the hierarchy of all spiritual preceptors of mankind. This agai is no different from the attitude of all other Hindu sectarian foun dations, whose inceptors have all acquired divine status, and ar in principle directly identified with the supreme deity. On th dogmatic side, the Swaminarayan theology is an almost unmodifie take-over from the modified-dualistic teachings of Ramanuj (eleventh century A.D.).

The Sikhs, with their simpler and highly formalized Gurumukl corpus of prayers form their canon, the *Guru Granth Sahib*, must b classed in the 'big tradition' whatever the origins of Sikhism wer three hundred years ago. They have their regular *kirtas* (litanies on Sundays, with a steady and large number of devotees, both male and female. There is no doubt that the attendance is more proportionate, between men and women, among the Sikhs than among any Hindu group.

Sikh women do not seem, on an average, to be as eager for domestic worship; the Panjabi Hindu women are less eager than the Gujarati and Cutchi women—the average time given daily to formal worship would be something between 1-2 hours among Gujarati women, and from between ten minutes to half an hour among Panjabi Hindu and Sikh women.

East African Hindus follow a great variety of sects of very different degrees of religious sophistication. Most of these sects hail from the middle of the sixteenth century A.D. and later, and there is hardly any adherence to the classical schools.

The doctrines directly inculcated in religious education—through processes of deutero-learning rather than through formal religious instruction which is almost non-existent in East Africa—were propounded by village saints, preachers, and reformers of the Indian middle ages; a majority of the East African Hindus, and almost all women follow the simple, rustic, ethical-cum-ascetical doctrines of those teachers. The sophisticated, however, have been more recently influenced by the teachings of the Hindu Renaissance, i.e., the reform movements of the last eighty years that spread all over India. Even from among these, some are decidedly on the pathological fringe, as the followers of Sat-Sai Baba, a saint of Muslim background but ascriptively a Hindu mystic, of the late eighteenth century. His present successor, who lives near Bangalore in South India, is reported to 'know everything that is said, done, and thought anywhere in the world', and to be able to cure all diseases which medical people have given up as beyond remedy. This cult is magicocentric, its votaries tend to go into mild stages of trance, which is remarkable as so far all the literature on Sai Baba has been published in English only; during their regular meetings, one person reads the deeds of Sai Baba in English and then translates it into Gujarati, sentence by sentence.

At Nakuru in Kenya, there is a Lohana shopkeeper, referred to as Hirji Baba Maharaj. He is approaching 70, a quaint looking man with a greenish turban of his own design. He has been travelling from place to place all over East Africa, and in about forty years he has won a following of several thousand Hindus, mostly Lohanas, Patels, and 'small *jati*' Gujaratis and Cutchis. He chants and interprets the Hindi Ramayana composed by Tulsidas,

a village-Brahmin of North India, who flourished in the sixteenth
century. Hirji Baba seems to be the only Hindu teacher who has
made some converts among Africans—there are about a dozen
Jaluo and Kikuyu followers, who have learnt Gujarati and Hindi
participate in the *bhajan* (litany), follow other Hindu ritual, and have
assumed Hindu names. A few years ago, a whole boat was
chartered by his devotees, whom he led to several shrines in India
and back. To any non-Gujarati Hindu, the concomitant ritual
seems pretty 'old-fashioned'—but when a modern East African
Panjabi uses this term in the context, it has the same feeling-tone
as the modern American use of 'sick'. Itinerant monks invited
to Hirji Baba's meetings—as well as to other religious functions
among the Gujaratis—are placed on an altar, worshipped through
arati (oil-lights waved around them in a circular motion as around
temple icons). Their feet are washed with milk and sweet water
the water distributed as *caranamrt* (a libation poured over the deity's
or the holy man's feet, literally, 'foot-nectar') and drunk for spiritual
merit and benefit. Such occasions are not rare and far between
they occur right around the main streets of Nairobi, Dar es Salaam
and Kampala.

While the hitherto mentioned groups form the majority of the
East African Hindu body politic, there is an increasingly large
number of people, distributed with varying density over all the
constituent linguistic and caste groups, who follow one or more of
the teachings of what I call the Hindu Renaissance, the modern,
English language-using simplification and popularization of the
scriptures by an eclectic, quasi-Sanskrit oriented, rhetorical 'big-
tradition' echelon of preachers beginning with Swami Vivekananda
at the turn of the century, and continuing today with an ever
increasing host of monastic and lay teachers and organizations
that have their headquarters in many parts of India, and—as with
the Ramakrishna Mission, the Divine Life Society, or the self-
Realization League, in western countries as well. Strangely enough,
East Africa is the only place with a sizable Hindu population,
where the Ramakrishna Movement has not established itself (it is
quite well established and influential in neighbouring South Africa);
one of the reasons may be the total absence of Gujarati- and Panjabi-
speaking monks in that organization, as all the Ramakrishna-
Vivekananda monks are Bengali or Dravidian speakers. The
honours are shared between the school of the late Swami Shivananda
Sarasvati of Hrishikesh on the side of naive religious appeal and,
for the religiously more astute, by the Sri Aurobindo *ashram* at

Pondicherry, which has become a world-wide movement. It is largely the Patel community that got enthused by it, and one of its leaders, now retired from active life, has moved permanently to the *ashram* in South India.

Swami Shivananda, of South Indian Brahmin descent, had been a medical practitioner in Malaya, saw the light and became a *sannyasi*; and set himself up at the foot of the Himalayan range in Hrishikesh on the upper Ganges, a centre of monastic activity in North-Western India. Within ten years he established a 'Forest University', wrote literally scores of books on religious topics, health, morals, and became by far the most successful popularizer of simplified, theistic, eclectic Hinduism which uses English as its tool of communication. He appealed to an audience that knew some English and no Sanskrit, or a vernacular only—all of his books and most of the periodical writings of his institution appear in the major Indian languages. They included Indian Government employees, officers in the armed forces, lawyers, schoolteachers, in short all the people with whom E. Shils[8] deals in his excellent study. Shivananda was prolific, pompous and puritanical, the ideal combination of the official culture of modern India, 'healthy' in the sense of stout and 'light-coloured', he fitted into the image of the Hindu hierophant. His followers do not object to the sanctimoniousness that is so disturbingly obvious to any critical reader, simply because there is no word, and hence no concept of this sort in modern Hinduism. He created the Divine Life Society, with followers in California and in Nairobi, in Bonn and in Dar es Salaam. Almost all educated Hindus in East Africa have some acquaintance, and most of them the profoundest admiration for the Shivananda movement. His teachings are perhaps most typical, comprehensive, and the most representative of the simplified 'big tradition' Hinduism that officially prevails in East Africa; a Hinduism which emphasizes bourgeois virtues, yogic and 'spiritual' exercises, a naive *mens sana in corpore sano* acceptance of all religions and all teachers of religion without explicit value comparison, and an eclectic reading of the most frequently translated texts of the Hindu tradition, especially the Bhagavadgita, though hardly any of the canonical Upanishads. Literally thousands of East African Hindus have made Swami Shivananda their *guru in distans*, although he never set foot outside India since he took up the monastic life. The fact that Hindus refer to him as the 'Himalayan Sage' or the 'living incarnation of the Divine' goes to show what ascriptive charismatic status can do. Hrishikesh is certainly no more in the

Himalayas than Arusha on Mt. Kilimanjaro.

By far the most sophisticated version of modern Hinduism available in East Africa is the Shri Aurobindo cult. Aurobindo and his spiritual consort '*la Mere*', a French Jewish woman who joined him many years ago, established fame through his English writings, and through the exquisitely organized *ashram* which combines healthy living with 'spiritual' life, meditation, yoga exercises, plain food, a euphoric atmosphere and a cosmopolitan flavour. Aurobindo himself, though Bengali by birth, never learnt his mother-tongue in a literate sense, and published all his writings in English, much more sophisticated but no less sancti monious than the writings of Shivananda and the other swamis of the Hindu Renaissance.

The Theosophical Society has made some headway in East Africa and there are Lodges in all the larger cities. Many theosophists are simultaneously admirers or followers of Aurobindo, as of Swami Shivananda. The 'esoteric' writings of Mme. Blavatsky are read and admired. Only English speakers are among the active theosophists, as few of the theosophical writings have been translated into Gujarati. On the ritualistic side, however, the theosophists continue their domestic worship according to their respective Hindu background. Whereas the Aurobindo cult has attained ritualistic status-pictures of Aurobindo and '*la Mere*' abound in Patel houses, and candles are lit in front of them in the style of regular Hindu worship—there are no pictures of Annie Besant, Blavatsky, or other founders of the Theosophical Society

The Jains are among the most wealthy and influential of the Gujarati- and Cutchi-speaking groups. The section which is particularly strong in East Africa, is the Visa Oshwal community which has the most autonomous and efficient educational institu tions, next in size and calibre only to the Ishmaili institutions of the Aga Khan. Although Jainism originally forbade agriculture as a profession that entails the taking of (microbic) life, the Visa Oshwals of Jamnagar, Porbandar and adjacent areas were originally farmers, though they came as tradesmen to East Africa. Jainism is an atheistic religion, it denies the authority of the Hindu scriptures but its ritual and its attitude towards life is very similar indeed especially to modern puritanical Hinduism. Most East African Jains are not too cognisant of the radical differences between Hindu and Jaina doctrine, and though their temples are separate, most Jains—especially women—invoke Hindu gods and goddesses along with the 'Tirthankaras', the semi-mythical founders of Jainism.

This about summarizes Hindu practice in East Africa. Prof. Hsu's otherworldly, unilateral orientation[9] finds full corroboration in the East African Indian outlook. Otherworldliness breaks through at every moment, and the pleasures of life are viewed with religious suspicion even by the many who indulge freely in them, creating highly dysphoric feelings of remorse and guilt. Hindus and Sikhs in East Africa who have made over a certain number of millions tend to stop eating meat and drinking alcohol even when they had been partaking of both in their less wealthy days.

After this rundown on the workings of applied religion and ritual in Indian East Africa, it now remains to describe the Hindu teachings as assumed by the communities. This is much easier and requires less bulk: Hinduism as prescriptive ideology is rather simple in the diaspora, and with the exception of literary involvements (Aurobindo, Theosophists, etc.) the idea part of East African Hinduism can be stated with ease. Unlike the lay Christian or the lay Muslim's ready answer to questions of the form 'what is a Christian' or 'what is a Muslim', the East African Hindu finds the corresponding definitional question somewhat embarrassing, for although he can give a discourse on what he thinks is *right* to do and to think, he cannot give a definition of Hinduism or of 'being a Hindu', because the theological apparatus essential for such a definition is lacking in East African parlance. The Eastern Mediterranean teachings are simple and on the lay level, of a piece. The Hindu teachings are not, unless those of a single school like the *Arya Samaj*, universalized, which is an unpalatable idea to all but the *Arya Samajis*. The average East African Hindu, particularly the younger ones, when asked this question would say 'My parents were Hindus, they told me I am a Hindu, but I really don't know what it means'. This, however, does not countervail a pervasive set of religious ideas held by the subjects. On the contrary, their articles of faith are readily enumerated: the East African Hindus believe—as did their forebears in India—in an all-pervasive divinity, usually appealed to as Vishnu, especially in his *avataras* (incarnations) as Rama and Krishna, or as Shiva, with or without his spouse (Devi, Jagadamba, Shakti, etc.) or the hypostasized World Mother alone, without Shiva. Divinity is also manifest in minor representations of a heroic, demoniacal, or human form like Hanuman, the monkey-warrior who assisted Rama in his recovery of Sita, the latter's spouse, herself an incarnation of the world goddess Lakshmi, Vishnu's eternal cosmic partner. Hanuman is both the epitome of chaste, unwed, loyal piety and

religious devotion (*bhakti*).   Along with it, all Hindus with the
exception of the *Arya Samajis* who are vehemently anti-anthropo-
morphic and iconoclastic—believe that divinity is both 'formless'
(*nirakar*) and endowed with anthropomorphic or theriomorphic
'form' (*sakar*) according to the spiritual needs and competence of
the devotees, but that the approach through 'form', i.e. through
one of the divine incarnations is easier and closer to the heart of
most 'common people'. The main text referred to and quoted from
is the *Bhagavadgita*, the most important, though non-canonical
text of the Hindu Renaissance.   Its extreme eclecticism appeals to
the modern Hindu, its implied herolatry adds to the appeal.   It
contains religious and quasi-ethical injunctions and provides a
definite code of living for the Hindu non-specialist.   The fact that
this text is non-canonical, and hence not a compulsory creed for a
Hindu, is hardly known to anyone in East Africa.   The emphasis,
especially amongst the Gujaratis and Cutchis, is on pronounced,
intensive devotional practice (*bhakti*, *bhajan* and *kirtan*—religious
litany and congregational worship in the home and in temples and
at casual places of assembly, in fellow-devotees' homes).   Most
East African Hindus are aware that there are many other ways of
propitiation of the divine apart from *bhakti* but then, following the
general tenor of the middle-class Hindu Renaissance, *bhakti* is
regarded as the best and the least extravagant, and does not presuppose the knowledge of Sanskrit and philosophy which is non-
existent in East Africa.

The relation between religion and life is just as intensive and
paramount among East African Indians as Hsu has seen it in India.
The quasi-pragmatical aspect of it, the direct impact of the
numinous on life in society is again expressed in that unique eclecticism which makes both the logician and the humanist nervous,
the theologian apprehensive, and the anthropologist delighted.
All East African Hindus assume that goods are dispensed on the
basis of *karma*, i.e. that life's sorrows and joys (but especially its
sorrows) are due to *purvasamskaras*—i.e., to the aggregate effects
of the individual's deeds and attitudes in past lives and in the present
life, and that their present attitudes and activities will determine
the course of things to come.   At the same time, most East African
Hindus *also* state that whatever happens to them is due to one's
taqdir (fate), 'Nothing can happen unless it is written on a person's
forehead'; 'Nothing happens which God has not fixed and decreed'.
These are sayings of wealthy, relatively well-read and 'modern'
Hindus in East Africa, quoted from conversations held in 1964.

The obvious contradiction does not occur to them unless it is pointed out by some itinerant scholar: either one believes that happiness and sorrow are due to one's own past actions and omissions, or contrariwise, that they are somehow predestined by an external force, divine or demoniacal. Historically, the latter notion is a direct bequest of Islam in India. The use of the Arabic, hence Islamic term *taqdir* in Hindu parlance does not strike the Hindu as a contradiction in terms, unless some outsider presses him into a logical-theological decision, which he is most reluctant to do.

Like all naively religious in the world, the East African Hindu assumes that all religions teach basically the same things—namely, rules for a moral life. The notion that morality might have to be separated from religion and that ethical themes are thematically distinct from religious teachings is totally foreign, horrifying and distasteful to him. The same holds for East African Indian Muslims, Jains, Sikhs and Catholic Goans. Most men, particularly the 'modern', claim eloquently that they 'don't care for religion', and that it is only their womenfolks and the very old who do; but this is sheer make-believe. The entire value system of the East African Indians is strictly religious, and there is no trace of a genuinely secular evaluation of moral situations. The conception of a rationally or intellect based morality or an ethical value orientation devoid of religious reference is as yet completely unthinkable to our subjects.

Very similar in proportion to the sister-groups in India, religion is one of the few permanent sources of relaxation and entertainment—and for the women, perhaps the only respectable one. There are Hindi 'cinemas' galore, there is drinking and card-playing at home and with friends and in the club, but from among 800 informants constituting a cross-section of the Hindu and Muslim Indian population of East Africa I found only four men and two women who were not fascinated by religious problems. These four were occidentally trained university lecturers and academic assistants at the various branches of the University of East Africa.

It is futile to talk about social customs in India without constant religious reference. There is no divergence from this nexus on the East African scene. There are no secular social institutions of an indigenous kind in India—sports-clubs, bridge-clubs, etc. and any voluntary associations of the type Hsu[9] denotes as 'clubs' are western imports; and without any modification, this holds for East African Indians. Men do join clubs, there is the 'Patel Club' in the bigger cities, setting itself apart from the conservative 'Patel

Brotherhood'—the former consciously emulating western club style. There is Rotary, Lions International, Round Tablers in all larger cities and the membership is on an average one fourth to one half Indian. There is the Masonic Lodge, which has a high percentage of Indian members. But none of these are indigenous, and one might even construe the desire to join a Lodge as a transmogrified form of ritual-seeking, not just of good fellowship or mutual aid, as with occidental joiners. Social life remains ritualistically directed life, regardless of whether ritual is openly performed by the women, or inveighed against by the 'modern' males who need a cathartic agent to compensate for the oppressive overt ritualism at home, when constantly exposed to occidental models of club-making or secular socializing.

Customs around the life-cycle are *ipso facto* religious in any Indian setting. Women do go to the hospital now for delivery, but most women over 40 had their first babies delivered by Indian midwives at their parental home. Most of the early childhood ritual is omitted, and remembered only by the older generation. The investiture of the boys with the holy thread (*jeneu*), indispensible in upper-caste India, is usually no longer performed as an isolable ceremony, but coincides with the young man's wedding—when the investiture is done a few days previous to his wedding. No one except the professional temple-priests (*purohit*) wears the thread after his wedding whereas the high-caste sister communities in India still observe the custom today. Even the East African Brahmin males—who form a tiny proportion of the total Hindu population—hardly wear the sacred thread. No one takes to the traditional fourth or monastic stage of life, but there is a strong admiration of men who have taken it in India, and who are invited as preachers.

Marriage rituals are quite unchanged from the Indian base: the Gujarati and the Panjabi groups conduct their weddings more or less as they do in India, with the basic rite—the circumambulation of the sacred fire, the seven steps, the ascending of the stone by the bride for 'firmness of the house' being identical for all Hindus. The groom's party (*barat*) arrives by car, and fortunately the young man is not made to approach the bride's house on horseback as he is required to do in India. Each community has its own *purohits* or priests, usually employed by the temple authorities of the various communities. Marriage is still an expensive business, the dowry system is strong and oppressive, resented by most, continued by almost all, and rejected, in a somewhat utopian fashion, by younger parents. An overwhelming majority of all marriages, Hindu, Sikh and Muslim, are still arranged by the parents, but the children have a veto to a far more real degree than in the Indian sister communities.

Death ritual is unchanged, too, though simplified, and the feeling of ritualistic pollution is all but non-existent. Hindus cremate their dead, in electric crematoria in the largest cities where open cremation is frequently disallowed by municipal regulation. The Hindu cremation grounds are usually close to the cemeteries of other communities. There are minimal obsequial observances, for which the temple priests may be called in. Only men over a certain age attend the cremation; young people and all women stay home and conduct *bhajan* (litany). The immediate kin of the deceased do not cook for a day, sometimes for as many as three days, and close friends do the cooking in their own homes bringing the cooked food to the mourners.

The interpersonal relations between men and women are as tense and obtuse as they are in India, and it is here that stagnation is almost complete. There is virtually no premarital romantic contact except among the very young who have gone to college or who have been employed in occidental-style firms; foreign-returned young people make it a point to be different, and there is some amount of dating, with the parents' consent; the Ishmailis seem to be the least inhibited relatively speaking in their dating patterns, and the coffee houses and restaurants in the larger cities are full of young Ishmailis, especially on Saturday mornings, eyeing each other with interest and wanting it to be known that they do so. Inter-caste marriages, as mentioned in an earlier context, are exceedingly rare, in spite of most peoples' claims to the contrary. There is a slightly higher proportion of cross-caste dating among the young emancipated.

In marriage, and among the male and female adult in any social situation, the mutual ignoring pattern is unchanged. There is complete avoidance—at least overtly—and there is no display of concern or tenderness of any sort between husbands and wives, which would be regarded not only as bad etiquette, but as bordering on the immoral. Here again, the Ishmailis are exceptional to a degree, one does see interested smiles and warmth between males and females in that community, but this is one reason why other communities—Hindu and even Muslim—tend to regard the Ishmailis as a whole as morally corrupt or at least suspect. Husbands simply do not and may not show any tender feelings to their wives *coram publico*, they have to use curt, terse language with them in front of others, particularly the elders in the house, and any ever so faint show of mutual affection is frowned at by the old, and pointed out as morally reprehensible. Daughters-in-law with a modern outlook who insist on having their husbands' attention in the joint house, are the epitome of wickedness in their in-laws' eyes.

An unmarried girl who acts in a matter-of-fact manner in the modern sense, as in taking employment in such technocentric organizations as television, radio, the Press, or sales promoting business, or even the mere fact that she went to school in Britain makes young men suspicious very much like their parents, about her eligibility as a wife. Even the most 'advanced' young men tend to bracket such girls as 'club-types', and once this nomenclature is applied to any girl, her marriage chances are profoundly jeopardized. This is a pattern of stagnation—for the Indian sister communities have by and large abandoned such preconceived notions, and it appears that young men in East Africa frequently perpetuate an evaluation pattern set by their grandparents in India. The identification of 'purity' with virginity is axiomatic, and naively uncritical even among completely westernized people. The young men's naivete about women and their notions of romantic love are in part created, and wholly reinforced by the Hindi movies which form the focus of East African Indian secular entertainment across all the groups constituting the Asian minority; Hindi movies are, incidentally, preferred by a sizable lower-middle and labour class majority of Africans, to British and American productions, and there are many Africans who hum and sing Hindi film tunes. The Hindi screen is full of totally unrealistic paste-and-cardboard romances, with male-female relationships as they never existed in India (or indeed elsewhere,) and emotional conflicts are resolved by a song or a dance or both. These film songs seem to inspire and inform most of the erotic conceptions of the Indian population, young *and* old—the former overtly and proudly in their parlance, the latter surreptitiously. As most young people can drive and can use their parents' cars, there is a fair chance to take out a girl once in a while and 'drive her around', and this process occurs usually, but by no means only, within the driver's caste. Prospective mates are allowed to enjoy such drives, or go to the movies. Indulgence of a mild sort amounts, on a cautious guess, to about 10 per cent, and though (American and British) movie-inspired kissing is good style, there is little necking and hardly any petting at such occasions; premarital full sexual intercourse among young adults of the same social and economic grouping is virtually non-existent, and its suggestion elicits shocked horror. Young men who studied abroad usually have had their sexual initiation overseas, but they do not apply it until they get married; courting an Asian girl without a view to a marriage but with a view to sexual consummation is rare, and if the chance arises, this western-informed, premarital consummation is not often carried through. Parents who have sent their children abroad for 'schooling' live under a constant fear that their offspring might not return or bring a European mate; frequently, mothers and fathers expect pledges of complete avoidance from their children before they send them abroad. A girl who is suspected of having lost her virginity, either abroad or at home, is not likely to find a marriage partner at all, regardless of her religious and caste background. The same, of course, does not apply to men. Unlike in puritanical circles in the western world, where a young man may indulge and be connived at with a knowing pat on his shoulders and a smirk, the young Asian who is known to have 'enjoyed' is censured with genuine rebuke, though he may be faintly and clandestinely admired by his own male peers. The elders then refer to him as having developed 'bad habits', which means that he has made or makes extramarital or premarital love and drinks—and nothing else; the notion that sex and drink go together as universally concomitant vices is so deep-rooted that the suggestion that some persons may enjoy the one to the exclusion of the other is met with complete unbelief. There are 'love-marriages', i.e. marriages not arranged by the parents, which constitute a negligible proportion of marriages in the higher income brackets and are virtually unknown in the lower income brackets. The male partner, especially among the 'modernized' and affluent, makes bold of the fact that he broke the old outmoded fashion to which the majority adheres.

Postmarital courtship follows an unvarying pattern—immediately after the wedding, the bride moves into her husband's home; marriage is consummated within the first week, but apart from the young men who have had some experience abroad, it usually takes from 6-7 months for the first pregnancy to occur. Honeymoon trips after the wedding are as yet quite unusual, and two Panjabi couples who did venture on an East African *safari* tour were talked about with some scorn as having been on 'Hari OM' or 'Hanuman'[10], and though young folks to be married would like to plan a honeymoon, the suggestion is usually received with some embarrassment. For about one year after her wedding, the young woman is supposed to—and usually does—wear expensive, colourful *saris* as part of the extended ritual. The Ishmailis form an exception once again, for due to a *firman* of the late Aga Khan no wedding dress must cost over 30 E.A. shillings, regardless of the financial status of the bride's family.

In the previous decades, the East African Indian birthrate tended to be slightly higher than that of the sister communities in India. The present generation, however, is very definitely conscious of the population problem, and the very acute problems of family growth in the present critical, transitional situation. There is a fairly pervasive intention among younger couples to limit the number of children to three or four, and most modern means of contraception are known and employed. Vasectomy has become known during the past few years, and about half a dozen men in some of the bigger cities casually told me that they had undergone the operation, or had seen to it that their wives underwent the parallel operation to prevent further conception.

One of the most positive features of East African Indian social life is the manner of child rearing. With a great majority of the total Asian population still living in a joint family setting, the rest being recent split-offs from larger units, the number of infants, toddlers and children, siblings and cousins, in a house of four rooms averages from three to six. They are brought up with great affection, and the boys with overly great indulgence. The patience of the adults and adolescents in the house—grandparents, parents, older siblings and cousins—with the screaming youngsters, particularly the boys, is absolutely amazing for anyone not reared in the Indian tradition. The only negative feature, fairly pervasive in all the constituent communities, is of no real pedagogical concern to the growing children, but it is a psychologically disorienting agent within the adult family: in continuation of the Indian tradition by which the grandparents assume considerably more right than the parents to handle and play with the young children, grandparents in East Africa tend to compete with the parents for the affection of the small children as well as for that of the pre-adolescents. The situation is particularly toxic when there is tension between the mother-in-law and her daughter-in-law; whenever the child acts up, the former tends to put the blame on the younger woman who, due to her lower position in the domestic hierarchy, cannot usually defend herself, especially as her husband tends to side quite openly with his mother against his wife. The methods of parental *vs.* grandparental competition for the children's affection are often quite insidious and they pervade almost all facets of daily relations within the house.

There is a definite preference for sons. Panjabi and Hindustani speakers, just like in India and Pakistan, called their little *daughters* 'beta', which means 'son'. This teknonymy is a North Indian one —when pointed out to an average audience in North India, the preference is usually admitted; in East Africa, it does not imply any emotional discrimination in the sense that girls are not wanted —here for once, the East African Indians clearly show some ideological advance—it is simply the linguistic left-over of an institutionalized Freudian slip and would probably be dropped if an effort were made. Fathers and grandfathers are extremely tender to their little sons and to their daughters, little and grown-up, mothers and grandmothers to both at all ages, and all males in the house to the female children. There is virtually no beating, although the threat of beating is often made as a corrective or deterrent.

The paternal attitude to sons, particularly the eldest son, changes when the boy reaches adolescence; the relation becomes formal, often stiff, and the two feel socially uncomfortable with each other. The same holds for the oldest brother and his younger sibling brothers—there is hardly any personal intimacy between them, but there are indications that there is a lot of floating hostility between the eldest brother—who is likely to be the head of the house when his father retires or dies—and his 'real', i.e., sibling brothers.

The Gujarati parent seems less indulgent than the Panjabi, particularly in matters of religious indoctrination, which is quite radical in Gujarati Hindu households. There may be a higher degree of secular disciplining among Panjabis, but religious and ideological training which the average Gujarati householder devolves on his children is virtually absent with the Panjabi Hindus and Sikhs. Gujarati parents expect their children—from toddlers to adolescents and young adults—to attend the evening prayers in the house, and by the time the child reaches school age small-congregational family prayer has become quite natural. Such procedure is rare with Panjabis.

The pattern is slightly different with the various Muslim groups. Ithna-Asharis and Bohras apply some pressure on their young to perform their prayers at least informally. The situation is different with the Ishmailis. Almost all of them, young and old, regard the *Jamatkhana* as their spiritual and social home and place of congregation, and the Friday visit is compulsory. The sermons are

combined with social meeting, fund-raising, auctioning of food
cooked by individual women in their homes and carried to the
Jamatkhana, where bachelors or people who just did not cook can
buy good home-cooked food, the proceeds of the auction going to
the poor-fund.   With the Ishmailis, the bringing up of the young
in the faith is a very gentle, unobtrusive, almost a playful procedure,
but it is absolute.

It is a mute question whether ritualistic purity in the manner
observed and stressed by anthropologists reporting on India proper
does at all apply to East African Hindus.   Precautions, actions,
and attitudes concerning ritualistic purity are at best vestigial.
Menstruating women do not participate in any religious activity,
and the Gujaratis usually stay out of the kitchen.   Women usually
—though not as invariably as in India—take their bath before
performing their formal worship in the house-shrine.   There is
none of the 'natural horror' of entering the shrine or performing
one's worship without a bath as is the case in the sister communities
in India.

The joint or extended family system is still the rule among the
Asian settlers.   In theory, 'modern people', that is people who have
passed their Senior Cambridge Examination—often regarded about
all a good settler ought to want and aspire for himself and his
children—tend to break away into nuclear groups, though the
intention is hardly ever formulated.   'There were too many people
in my father's house—so we moved into one of our own', or some
such statement is most usually made as an explanation.   Very
often, younger brothers rejoin their father's or elder brother's
joint household, and even where a genuinely nuclear family has
been formed, there is constant upward visiting, i.e., the younger
brother and his wife visiting the senior joint house.   Younger,
unmarried but adult brothers tend to join such new, spacier set-
ups, though such cases have become countable only in very recent
years.   There is no doubt a great desire, among the younger generation, to nuclearize the family system.

In the majority of joint set-ups, the average number of couples
under one roof is 2-3 among the Panjabis, and 2-4 among Gujaratis,
irrespective of their religion; again, the Ishmailis are moving away
into a more radically nuclear ecological form, as the late Aga Khan's
scheme of providing a house for each family, on a co-operative
tenant-into-owner basis is taking effect increasingly; this of course
might, in theory at least, work for a reinstatement of a joint household system, except that these tenements are really too small to

harbour larger family units. As in the classical Indian system, a 'joint household' simply means a senior man and his wife, their sons with their wives, their unmarried sons, and the unmarried daughters, who move away into their own virilocal setting when they marry.

Separate cooking among the various couples is rare in East Africa. One woman, usually the wife of the eldest son, supervises the cooking which is frequently done by African servants.

It is impossible to make a general assessment of interpersonal relations with respect to the degree of amity and discord, except in such socially structured relations as mother-in-law to daughter-in-law, oldest brother to younger brothers, etc. The father-oldest son relation seems to me more strained, though less overt among the Gujarati than among the Panjabi groups, whereas the latter are more overt but possibly not so intensively negative. Younger sons, and especially the latecomer male in the family, tend to get away more easily; as they are not expected to take over the father's responsibility, there is no high degree of potential competition, and their age often makes them equal with the oldest grandchildren, which adds tenderness and indulgence to the parental treatment of the very youngest direct offspring. As to the oldest son's relations to his *father*, I would concur with G.M. Carstairs statement[11] about the father-son relationship among Rajputs in Rajasthan, that 'the son does not have a psychologically independent sex life as long as his father lives'—even though the son may have several children. The feeling-tone of this statement applies to East African Hindus, with the exception of families where the fathers have already had occidental education or experience. The elder sons' relations with their wives in the house during his father's lifetime form a parallel extension: the sons do not have a psychologically independent sexual existence, oldest sons tend to be quiet, almost catatonic in the presence of their wives *en face* their fathers, they will not joke, will not dare to show any interest or affection for their wives; neither will they address their wives except to pass on domestic orders of the 'go and fetch . . . . .' type. In company of guests, oldest sons will answer 'yes' or 'no' if any questions are directly put to them, and they will not usually inaugurate a conversation themselves, in the paternal presence. Sons openly side with their mothers against their wives, and even some 'modernized' young men make bold of this fact. 'Women should have a secondary place in society', is not just a facile statement of the Rotary Club in-between lunch-and-speech conversation type, but a very germane reflection of the consanguinity syndrome in Hindu society.

Interpersonal relations with outsiders are a much more positive and pleasant matter. What strikes any student of East African Indian society, be he a casual visitor or a skilled observer, is the literally boundless hospitality of one and all toward the guest and the stranger. This goes for all communities with the possible exception of the Goans who due to their emulative 'European' style of living seem to feel that it is not good manners to feed one and everybody who comes by. They try to view guests on western models of modified hospitality: guests come invited only—in crass contradistinction to the Hindu view: the Sanskrit word for 'guest' is *atithi*, literally, 'one who comes without an appointment'. With all other communities, Hindu, Jain, Sikh or Muslim, refusal to treat a guest—any guest, not only a member of the community of the prospective host—to food and drink, and if required, to stay, is unthinkable. I conducted highly structured tests to check this radical hospitality and found it proved in all cases.

From an aesthetical viewpoint, living conditions are in no way better than with the equivalent economic groups in India. There is no improvement in artistic choice and taste. Most houses, cutting across all the Indian communities, decorate their interior with the Ravi Varma type oleographs and polychrome representations of gods, goddesses, Gandhi, Nehru, Vallabhai Patel, Sabhas Chandra Bose, kings and queens of the Hindu pantheon, film actresses from the Indian screen, sectarian and national Hindu leaders from the past 400 years, and an occasional photograph of Queen Elizabeth and Prince Philip, or even Elvis Presley stuck into the frames of the aforesaid products. The walls are replete with cheap chintz, and the oleographs themselves are perfectly ghastly, super-realistic, gaudily-coloured and embarrassingly banal. The choice has little to do with the economic level, for these artifacts are found among millionaire industrialists and the poorest *fundis* alike. Paper flowers abound on the tables and windowsills, even when the garden around the house produces fine specimens *en masse:* these seem to be reserved for the house-shrines only, though even their paper flowers tend to outnumber the natural plants. From among four of the leading Asian industralists in East Africa, only two families have genuine, elegant and refined Indian and European art in their residential premises.

The rooms of the affluent are overloaded with items of the same spurious kind, and the secret of empty spaces as a token of genteel living is not known, and the suggestion frowned upon.

In all Indian houses in East Africa, almost all living and bedrooms have photographs of the inmates of the house hung up or propped against chimney pieces and horizontal surfaces; the wedding photos of the oldest and the other senior couple is an invariable addition to the domestic gallery.

The standards in the other arts are equally poor. The Indian programme of the Voice of Kenya blares Hindi film music through many hours of the day, with classical and other good Indian music occupying a very small part of the total musical broadcasts. Phonographs are owned by almost everyone, with large collections of shellac records with almost 100 per cent 'filmi' music and there is a certain amount of scorn directed at the very few who would listen to or introduce good Indian music into their homes. As opposed to the All India Radio programmes which have been creating a well-nigh universal taste for good music in India in spite of initial protests, there is no movement to improve the standards of musical taste in Indian East Africa. There are one or two hapless teachers of Indian classical music and classical dance (*Bharata Natyam, Manipuri,* and the 'oriental' eclectic type) in the three largest cities, but their clientele is negligible in number and influence. There is still a feeling among most parents that it is not quite proper for a girl to learn dancing, and that it is a 'waste' for a boy to learn music. As a particularly noxious side-effect of this puritanism which is rampant among the East African Indian elders we notice the phenomenon that once music and dance do come upon the scene—either vicariously through records and radio and film, or through occasional attempts by the daughters of the house, no distinction of any sort is made, and with a shrug, there is 'dance' in the house, with no differential judgment between *Bharata Natyam* and the Twist, and none between the sentimentalized film music and a classical *khayal.* Most of the young people who have gone through Senior Cambridge and who have 'mixed', know the Twist and other recent imports, and they love it; as in India in this decade, in saree or *sawar-kamiz* or slacks, the Twist has come to stay; *Bharata Natyam* has hardly arrived. Virtually none of the dance-and-music loving Indians of East Africa—I am using these epithets facetiously—would be able to distinguish a sequence of *Bharata Natyam, kathak,* and *Manipuri,* from 'filmi' dance. These un-pleasant features have to be pointed out in view of the fact that the sister communities in India, on the same and on lower economic levels, have taken quite extensively to the study and the practice of the genuine Indian fine arts.

Most Hindus in East Africa, challenged about the inferiority of religious paintings and oleographs in their temples and their homes, react with a shrug and with statements to the effect that 'pictures of God inspire us to be religious'—references to the need of aesthetical quality within the religious iconographic framework are not understood.

The East African Indian cuisine is no different in essence, from that of the sister communities in India and Pakistan. The Gujarati Hindu groups eat highly spiced, watery and largely vegetarian food with lots of chutneys, turmeric and sugar, cooked exclusively in oil. Khoja Ishmaili food and other Muslim groups eat spicy food with plenty of fish and meat, with the exception of pork—though a small percentage of the younger, especially the more 'advanced' Ishmailis do occasionally partake of it—whereas other Muslim groups are strict about this classical avoidance. The Panjabis eat simple, not too spicy, relatively wholesome dishes, cooked in *ghee* at all times; their staple is *roti* (hot flat wheat-cakes of whole wheat, '*chappatis*' in the old British Indian terminology), the staple of the Gujaratis is rice and *rotli*, a smaller, and oil-baked version of the Panjabi *roti*. Almost all Panjabis, Hindu, Muslim and Sikh eat meat (with the exception of beef), though strict *Arya Samajis* and most women over 50 do not. The most highly modernized visit European-style restaurants in the cities; those who do usually do not ask questions about the zoological provenance of the meat: quite a few Hindus who frequent restaurants believe, or profess to believe, that 'steak' is made of mutton, and 'hamburgers' of ham.

There is a strong stigma on the consumption of any alcoholic drink, among all communities except the Goans. A high proportion of Asian men drink whisky, the *par excellence* drink and the epitome of drink in general, but only a small number of the women under 40 join their husbands after some initial reluctance in the first years of marriage. Fathers encouraging their daughters to share a drink are totally unthinkable.

The meat situation is more complex—among all Hindus, there is a stigma on meat eating, even though most of the meat eaters make no secret of it. Most of the Gujarati Hindus and Jains are strict vegetarians except that many of the young among them have modified their habit into the 'eggarian' variety—for on a strict count, meat, fish and egg are all 'meat' in the Hindu tradition.

Most men smoke cigarettes, very few smoke cigars and pipes. Hardly any woman smokes, and even among the youngest, Britain-returned and most 'advanced', only a few would smoke, with the exception of Goan women who often do. Sikh men do not smoke, as Sikhism forbids it quite rigorously. But Sikhs who shave off to 'modernize' usually take to smoking like other Hindu males.

Everybody drives cars, young and old, male and female. Only twenty years ago, very few women drove and the ones who did had to brave universal censure—but since World War II, large numbers of Indian women in East Africa have taken to driving and do it as naturally as women in the western world. In fact even the untrained observer who compares city life in India and in East Africa will notice this as a striking—though sociologically hardly a very significant—feature; very few women in urban India drive cars; many Indian women in East Africa do. This is not only due to the economic difference—among economically equal urban groups in India, there is still a latent opposition to women who 'get around too much', and the car is the epitome of urban 'getting around'.

The contrast between the older and the younger generation is enormous and must be an indispensable final topic of this study. It is rather difficult to assess differences in the degree of contrast between the various constituent groups. Stagnation is stronger among the Gujaratis than among the Panjabis, but least strong with the Khoja Ishmailis—it is perhaps not too incautious a statement to say that the cultural and ideological discrepancy between young and old is stronger in the more emancipated groups, and the least marked among more stagnant groups as the Jain Shahs and some Cutchi Hindus. The older generation complains about the lax morality of the young and even doctors and other professional men over forty attempt to keep a strict watch over the 'morals' of their sons and, *a fortiori*, their daughters. Just as in India today, 'morals' has a purely sexual connotation, with a much weaker anti-spirituous and anti-gambling-and-dissipation undertone. A man or a woman of 'good morals', who does not have 'bad habits', is one who does not indulge in any non-marital nor too much in marital sexual activity (the woman who involves her husband too much, or is suspected of doing so, sexually—is immoral by extension and assumption). Drinking *vs.* teetotalling forms the second and much less critical criterion of 'morality' in the Indian value hierachy, unsuccessful gambling the third and weakest. A 'good' girl or boy would be one that stays at home, eats food with his parents, does not go 'to cinema' too often or with people not known to the parents, and does not ponder any sort of interpersonal relation with a non-kin person of the other sex. An 'immoral' youngster, in the eyes of the older generations, would be one who stays out of the house and does not tell the parents where he has been, indulges or is thought to indulge in romantic activities or tastes, and takes drinks outside the house.

It is important to bear in mind that there is no difference in the intrinsic value-judgments of young and old. When the young rebel, they do so by doing, or pretending to do or fancy the 'immoral things'; they do not criticize fundamentals, i.e. the implicit value judgments, for they feel about as guilty as their parents about these censured indulgences.

As indicated above, the cultural and psycho-socially significant distinctions between old and young are smaller and more trivial than the unskilled observer would think. Young and old women drive cars; young men drink hard liquor, so do old men; young and old men, and many women, have taken to meat eating; young men and women, returned from abroad, or exposed to patterns of western living, meet at parties, go to the movies, dress in what the last generation would have called immodest garments, might do the Twist or engage in occasional necking; young men might boast of not going, or having never been to a temple—but so do old men. The older women's complaint that the young have abandoned religion is purely rhetorical, as their own husbands except for a small percentage, never practised religion in any ritualistic fashion. Yet this is not the point; the entire value-system is unilaterally directed to and informed by the religious lore. A Panjabi Hindu doctor in Kenya, trained in Britain, who has 'never been to a temple' once told me 'I know nothing about religion, I am a worldly man, I am not interested in religion, in the relation between the *Atman* and the *Brahman*, in rebirth and the question whether our actions depend on past impressions or whether God dispenses them, in the possibility of the cessation of birth and rebirth through yogic contemplation, in *Karma*, the *avataras*—', elaborating his denial in precise theological language; by the time he was through he had listed about all the main teachings of the Hindu theology. The irony of this example might be brought out for the western reader by an analogy of the very unlikely English physician telling an investigating anthropologist 'I am not at all interested in the Christian religion—they call me a Christian, but I know nothing about periochoresis, traducianism, the relation of the Son and the Paraclite, the eucharist'. The Indian doctor's statement is typical, the putative British colleague's very improbable.

In one point, however, there is no doubt that the younger generation diverges radically from the older. Although, as was shown in some detail, young men, and women have not entered inter-caste marriage liaisons in statistically significant proportions, they all favour it in principle, where the older are either overtly or covertly negative and antagonistic. One gets the impression that those among the older who verbally encourage inter-caste marriage would rather see others than their own kin enter such liaisons. Women over forty hardly ever support the idea and the frequent statements of the form 'whatever makes my son or daughter happy, he or she should do' is modified, under guided query, to indicate that cross-caste liaisons would not make the parents happy, though they would resign themselves to the situation should it arise.

Our concluding theme is the impact of western culture and organization on the Asian minority. It is overwhelmingly evident that western impact on the technological side is much stronger here than in India and Pakistan. On the ideological and on the cultural side, however, there can be no such unequivocal statement. The impact of western models on the various Asian communities is highly diversified in every except in the somewhat naive sense that 'all Asians' have better education, better houses and better chances. If we arrange the degree of acculturation to western models—apart from technological models where there is no distinction between the constituent communities—in a descending order of assimilation, the Khoja Ishmailis would rank on top, closely followed by Panjabi Hindus and Muslims, Sikhs, Gujarati Hindus (Lohanas, Patels, 'small' castes), Bohra Muslims, Ithna-Ashari Muslims, Visa Oshwal Jains and Shahs. This scale is purely exploratory and somewhat impressionistic, and I would not insist on a fixed hierarchy of assimilation and acculturation to western influence.

It must not be forgotten that the corpus of western influence is itself very limited in scope. No scholars, humanists and high-class British writers were among the East African white expatriates, and no top-level intellectual societies on the London, Oxbridge, and discursive Anglo Saxon salon-level were created that could have had an enculturating influence on the Asians. The British who came to East Africa were government servants, soldiers, farmers or businessmen—and apart from some occasional visiting anthropologists, archaeologists, and other scientists who came 'to the field', and who taught and teach in uneven density at the various institutions of what is now the University of East Africa—the British settler's pastimes were hunting and *safari*, golf and tennis, sports

and sundowners rather than discursive thought, intellectual conversation, Bach and such other activities that might disseminate
sophistication.   The Indians in East Africa have not had the benefit
of direct contact with the British and European intellectual
world, and those who went and go abroad for studies, do so with
narrowly set targets: the medical or dental profession, law, perhaps
engineering; none of these professions or the preceding training
are culture-giving *per se:* it is quite possible, and rather easy, to
take a medical degree in London without ever having heard anything about modern British literature and philosophy, and the fine
arts, etc.; of some fifty England-returned professionals I asked,
all of whom having spent a minimum of three years in Britain,
two had gone to the Albert Hall, and one to Covent Garden, though
all had 'seen' the British Museum, whatever that means.   It would
for these reasons be unfair to the Asian and the western elements
that coalesced in East Africa to stipulate a humanistic or aesthetically
discursive climate where there never was any institution of
precedence.

   The values held by the average British and European expatriate
population are intellectually naive; they range from traditional
Christian to pragmatic-secular values and the slightly more sophisticated and better-read attitudes of the British judges and higher
magistrates whose contact with the Indians was not dense and
sufficient for the devolvement of any intellectual interest to the
minority at large.   Young men read little except technical books
for their professional advancement, some novels, some Shakespeare,
etc. for their Senior Cambridge—but not after—and almost no
modern literature; this is not true about the peer generation of the
sister groups in India, where T.S. Eliot, D. H. Lawrence, and even
Kafka are being read along with the time-honoured Tennyson and
Dickens.   Visiting roughly one hundred houses of upper government servants and businessmen of all Indian communities, I have
seen but three book collections exceeding one hundred items of a
discursive or belletristic type.   Pious literature in English and
Gujarati abounds, but that was bought by the more directly religious
minded last generation.   Paperbacks are read, American and
British mysteries, the sexy penny-novel, amateur motoring and
engineering, Readers Digest are littered around the bed and
living rooms of many English-reading houses.   The Dale Carnegie
kind of 'how to be successful' literature is bought and read, and
some sex-technique and happy-marriage literature is found in some
of the most unexpected pious homes.   The impact of formal edu-

cation on the early school and the high school level acquired in British modelled private schools and, to a lesser degree, at the non-parochial public schools often creates a suspense or a break-down of communication between the adolescents and the elders at home who have not been exposed to this pedagogical model. There is a marked difference in this respect between the above type of schools and the Asian parochial schools (Ishmaili, Arya Samaj, Sanatan Dharm, Jain, etc.) where religious values are directly instilled as a more or less official part of the curriculum. These children seem to remain ideologically closer to their elders. Inter-viewing several boys and girls studying at the most fashionable and expensive schools which had not admitted Asians before *uhuru*, the following points seemed to emerge—the interviews were conducted separately and the subjects did not know each other: there is very little or no rapport with those members of their im-mediate and distant kin who had been brought up under the orthodox or conservative tradition transferred from India; there is close identification with the Asian, European, and less so with African peers who go to the same schools and who are taught in scholastic standards of the British model schools, with western cultural values guiding their staff and the text used. Kinship ties are accepted as inevitable, but with considerable grudge, and interfamilial personal relations continue only with those who have themselves adopted western educational values.

It is only the last generation that has undergone purely western-style formal education; the elders who are still in charge of the majority of Asian households have had hardly any formal education, and if they did, it was of the Indian parochial type, thoroughly suffused with Hindu or Muslim religious values which were thought to be universally valid and beneficial for the growing-up generations at the time of settlement.

By and large, the older generation still identifies occidental impact with loose, latently immoral and ethically degenerate and undesirable living. The most direct proof is the almost completely negative moral judgments the non-Ishmaili Indians have formed about the Ishmailis, the latter being the epitome of western culture in an Asian milieu, in the image of the Hindus and conservative Indian Muslims. The idea that the western model conduces to promiscuity, drink, laxity in general, and atheism is fairly pervasive with the older generation, and not infrequent with people between 35 and 45. The younger generation—between 20 and 40 exposed to western education since their childhood is trying hard to assimilate whatever it can cognitively perceive as not injurious to their self-image: modern cars, British and American movies, occasional occidental diet and restaurants, with family, friends, or surreptitious visits to coffee houses, etc. with a peer of the same or the opposite sex, with the acceptance in principle of individual, not caste-directed courtship.

Kitchen utensils, cutlery, crockery, etc., are entirely occidental, the large size metal *thali* which serves as the food-plate in India in the sister communities of the East African groups today, has been all but abandoned; most people still can use their hands for eating, but they do it with some embarrassment and prefer the use of knife and fork. For large-scale ritualistic occasions, the *thali* and the fingers are occasionally used, particularly among the more orthodox Gujarati. Houses are built very much as among the sister communities in India, on the basis of income, though not diffusely in the various communities; Gujarati Hindus tend to save money and invest, and their wealth can hardly ever be predicted from the looks of their houses, furniture, etc. Panjabis tend to spend much of what they earn on pleasant dwellings, with relatively little worry about long-range investments and savings.

Most Asians are quite gadget minded, TV, radio, transistorized and other, photography and cinematography are popular and frequent pastimes. The posed group is still the only known and accepted technique, the family album a compulsory chore for the guest.

In conclusion it must be said that western impact provides the form rather than the content of modern living among the Asian minority. This should be understood in a structural sense; it is not that, say, Indian food is eaten from European crockery, or that a battery-operated halo resolves around the icon in some Hindu temples—all this is true and amusing, perhaps amazing but not really important. But there is hardly any direct enjoyment of value-free food, drink and sex or the other goods of an emancipated, open society, as appurtenances to the sort of detached eudaimonism which many Indians in East Africa could afford. There is no self-criticism in any fundamental cultural sense, no self-persiflage, hence little sense of humour: loud laughs and practical jokes, emotional ebullience under drink, and occasional vernacular gibes where the *cochonerie* is taken for a punchline—these are the notions of a sense of humour, very much like in India, though an analytical, self-persiflaging generation of writers and thinkers is emerging there. The stylistic and ethical ennui of verbal pompousness, religious and rhetoric sanctimoniousness, and kin-bound complacence is not known, its suggestion not understood except by a few college teachers and their very narrow circle of peers.

It might seem a bit dismal to conclude this study on a basically pessimistic note; but I do not see how this can be avoided, as the hallmark of modern culture in its ideological sense—humanism, self-reliant, kinship-free planning, autonomous value judgments, etc. inclusive—is secularism; this has not transpired to the Asians of East Africa. Nationalism of the Indian or the now-let's-be-African type permeates the words and the thoughts of their finest leaders, non-secular, basically religious morality the rest. Modern technology is foisted on all this, but then there is no contradiction between any technology and any personal ideology. For all this, no one can blame the Asians; there simply was a lack of precedence for acculturation. The West to which the Indians of East Africa have been and are exposed, is not the West of Mozart, Picasso and Bertrand Russell, but the West of the tea and sisal estate manager or expert, and the government officer whose intellectual and golf handicaps are very disparate indeed.

References

1. The author's research on culture change among the Indian minority in East Africa was jointly sponsored by the National Institute of Mental Health of the U.S. Department of Health, Education, and Welfare and by the East African Studies Programme of the Maxwell School of Public Affairs and Citizenship at Syracuse University, New York· The comprehensive results of this research will be published in book form in a separate publication at a later date.

2. David Pocock, ' 'Difference' in East Africa: a study of Caste and Religion in Modern Indian Society', *Southwestern Journal of Anthropology* XIII/4, 289-300; 'Inclusion and Exclusion: A Process in the Caste System in the Gujarat'; *S.W.J.A.* XIII/I, 19-31.

3. *Clan, Caste and Club*, van Nostrand, New York and London, 1963.

4. M. N. Srinivas, McKim Marriott, S. C. Dube, M. Opler, Milton Singer a.o.

5. The East African Jains belong to the Visa Oshwal and Navnit Vanik castes. The former were farmers and landholders originally, the latter traders.

6. This terminology has been used for about two decades by Indian and British-American anthropologists like Redfield, Srinivas, Milton Singer, McKim Marriott and others. Roughly, the 'big traditions' are the religious-literary parts of any of the world's great religions. The 'little traditions' are the non-codified, pre-systematic or non-systematic modes of worship and ritual, witchcraft and sorcery, faith-healing, under the auspices of particularized ritualistic deities and demons, usually of rustic provenance. Whereas the functionaries of the 'little tradition', often belong to the pathological fringe, the priests of the 'big tradition' are literati, who handle the official version of the scriptures and the ritual. The two traditions, however, overlap at every step in India.

7.   vd. Hilda Kuper, *Indian People in Natal*, University Press, Natal 1960; there are extensive descriptions of possession, divination and kindred occurrences in that area, though Mrs. Kuper does not use the 'big-tradition-little tradition' tool as a heuristic device.

8.   Edward Shils, *The Intellectual Between Tradition and Modernity: The Indian Situation*. Mouton & Co., The Hague, 1961. The book, like most critical studies of modern Indian culture, has been vehemently criticized in India.

9.   Francis L. K. Hsu, *Clan, Caste and Club*, van Nostrand, London, 1963. This is by far the most perceptive study of caste and religion in Hindu India, and supersedes most previous research to date.

10. A phonetic play on the English word, 'Hari OM' is the Sanskrit formula at the beginning of the big tradition prayers and of many invocations. 'Hanuman' is the name of the devout monkey-warrior of the Ramayana, known to every Indian as a most venerable hero of semi-divine status. The fact that these highly elated terms are used goes to show, by a process of psycho-linguistic overcompensation and vindictiveness, how unpleasant the idea of a newly wed couple enjoying itself away from the man's prescribed parental home is to the conservative.

11. G. M. C. Carstairs, *The Twice Born*, Hogarth Press, London, 1958.

3. A Political Survey

Yash Tandon

Introduction

Historical truth is not simply a matter of fact: to grasp it the imagination must be aroused. But sometimes events move faster than imagination can keep pace with. Such is the case with Africa where one is likely to lose not only the perspective of time but even that of space: a century or so of colonialism over an area of about ten million square miles has unfolded in a matter of a few years.

Because of this factor of historical perspective, and the fact that the subject of this paper is too close to current events, the account is bound to be, to a certain extent, impressionistic, and therefore perhaps, controversial. This, however, is not an attempt at political introspection by a representative Asian. If there is a bias that the writer must confess to, it is towards an attempt at academic professionalism. Based on a discreditable amount of documents, or on documents, and on personal interviews by the writer, the paper does not claim to provide a full treatment of the political history of the Asians in East Africa since 1945. Rather the aim is to take from this history the broad trends and major factors which appear to be relevant to an understanding of it. The subject matter is accordingly divided into four themes: the nature of the content of Asian politics; the nature of the conduct of Asian political participation; African nationalism and the Asian response; and finally Asian politics in independent East Africa.

The Nature of the Content of Asian Politics

It can quite categorically be stated that the great majority of the Asians in East Africa never actively participated in politics, if by participation in politics we mean in the Aristotelian sense, the exercise of rational thinking in a public discussion over controversial political problems. Rather they, both as a community and as individuals, reacted to politics and to political events with the crudest animal instincts of survival and security. This can be witnessed

by the alternate waves of optimism and pessimism that betook
them in recent years whenever a political speech by an African
leader seemed to threaten their security or to preserve it. For a
large part, they were content with the existing peace; their brand of
political participation was intermittent and sporadic depending on
occasions when their peaceful existence appeared to be challenged.

Serious politics has been a business of no more than a few
individuals. What motivated these few to participate actively in
politics is anybody's guess. There is evidence to show that there
existed, at least in the British days, some correlation between being
a member of the Legislative Council, and improving one's business
prospects or professional clientele. This is not surprising: one's
prestige and status improved with being a member of the Legislative
Council, whether one was handpicked by the British as in the early
days, or, as later, elected by one's community. The reason for joining
politics, in most cases, was primarily personal. The function of
presenting 'the Asian point of view' (if there was one) was secondary
and incidental. With the Africans the reason for joining politics,
though partly personal, was also strongly influenced by the need
to force the pace of political evolution in these territories. With
the Asians, again with the exception of a few, the need to take a
stand on measures of political evolution came as a necessity,
sometimes unpleasant, after joining the Legislative Council rather
than as a contributing reason for it.

Why is it that a great part of the Asian population in East Africa
never consistently played an active role in politics? Illiteracy,
which in large part explains the non-participation in politics by
the African majorities, hardly explains the Asian position. We
must therefore look for some other explanation.

The orthodox explanation, with perhaps a degree of truth in it,
is that the Asians came to East Africa principally to trade and not to
rule. This explanation has a virtuous undertone; they, in other
words, came to East Africa not with the imperialist motives that
had driven the Europeans to scramble for Africa, but with purely
economic motives. Applying the push and pull theory, it was for
most of them the push imparted by the relative economic poverty
in their countries of origin, and the pull of brighter economic
prospects in East Africa, that were instrumental in persuading
them to part painfully with relatives and friends and undertake
a long sea voyage to an unknown continent. There were some who
came, or more correctly, were brought as indentured coolies to
build the railways, yet here again the economic aspect of the push

and pull theory was the operative factor. As far as the Europeans are concerned, the paramount factor was political not economic. The Marxian thesis of colonies for the economic gain of the colonial powers is not strictly applicable in Africa.

Is it then that the lack of Asian participation in East African politics can be accountable by the fact that the Asians who came to East Africa were mostly traders and businessmen? If it is, it then becomes difficult to explain why their brothers in British Guiana, in Fiji, in Malaysia and in South Africa were not equally restrained in their political activities. After all, their immigration into these countries was as much motivated by economic, rather than political, considerations as the Asian immigration into East Africa. If anything, the proportion of 'coolie-immigrants' to pure 'trader-immigrants' was considerably larger in these territories than in East Africa, and politically therefore they should have been less sophisticated than the Asians in East Africa. We must therefore look for some other explanation.

A second explanation, as naive as the above one, is that the Asian in diaspora is a meek gentleman not concerned about politicking in a foreign land. The evidence in Fiji, in British Guiana and in other places contradicts this theory as well.

A third explanation is that the Asians could not take part in politics because the East African territories were administered on a colonial (or protectorate or trust territory) basis by an imperial power, the British, who tolerated politics on their own terms only. Admittedly, an imperial régime imposes restrictions on the political activities in its colonies (the British sense of democracy and freedom of speech hardly ever crossed the Channel), and for a community, which was itself an immigrant trading community and at that a distinct race, the practical effects of a colonial rule over their political activities must have been both physically as well as psychologically inhibitive.

Although there is something in this explanation, it does not fully explain the morality of the Asian position. Laws against political demonstrations are no reason why demonstrations should not nevertheless take place if one truly believed in the cause of justice. Colonial laws hindered but could not altogether prevent political activities in India, or among the Africans in East Africa. The political quietude of the Asians in East Africa must therefore have some other reasons.

The first of these reasons is that the Asians were a relatively privileged class in East Africa. They were, of course, denied certain privileges, for example, ownership of land in the Kenya Highlands and attainment of positions of top grade in the civil service, yet they had virtually a free hand in the main occupation that interested the bulk of them—trade and commerce. There was, therefore, no good reason for them to spurn the British rule.

The second reason was that even if the Asians were to act the revolutionaries in the political struggle for independence, the prize was certainly not political power. They could never hope to seize power from the hands of the British, the way the Indians in Fiji and in British Guiana could. This was fully understood by every Asian in East Africa.

It was the tacit acknowledgement on the part of the Asians in East Africa of this limitation on their political aspirations that exerted a sobering influence on too open a manifestation of political radicalism—again barring a few farsighted individuals. The reluctance to participate actively in politics cannot therefore be explained exclusively in terms of the commercial interests of the Asians in East Africa, or in terms of the nature of the colonial rule. Two other factors were at least as significant: the fact that they had nothing in particular to shout against, since the prevailing peace and order under the British was good enough for their purposes; and the fact of the silent acceptance of the reality of power in East Africa.

Why was the attainment of political power in the territories of East Africa an ideal not within the grasp of the Asians? An understanding of the reasons for this, and the effects it had on the political behaviour of the Asians, is important in any assessment of their role in East African politics.

The first important reason is, of course, the plain arithmetic of numbers. Constituting, as they did, never more than $1\frac{1}{2}$ to 2 per cent of the population, the Asians could never hope to hold water in any bid for power the way their Asian counterparts in British Guiana and in Fiji could, where their numbers constituted about 50 per cent of the total populations.

But in politics numbers in themselves do not constitute the full answer to the problem of power, as evidenced by the history of the British (and other colonial powers') rule over populations vastly superior in number to their own, and as evidenced by the ability of dictators to rule over their countries with nothing more than police methods.

Thus where the authority to rule is not based on superior numbers,

it is based on superior power. The sanctions behind the British
rule in Kenya, Uganda and Tanganyika resided not in Nairobi,
Kampala or Dar es Salaam but in London. Ultimately, it was
the authority (and what goes with authority: control of the law, the
police and the army) which emanated from London that could
sustain the continued rule by the white minorities in these territories
over their subject races vastly superior in numbers to their own.
The point of this observation is borne out by subsequent history,
particularly of Kenya, of the gradual withdrawal of the sanctions
apparatus by London and the consequent almost overnight crumb-
ling of the power of the white minorities.

Sanctions were therefore an important ingredient of the European
power in Africa, and an element completely lacking on the Asian
side. It may be a controversial point for historians, but it is not
too difficult to believe that had the Asians in East Africa a sanctions
machinery to back any bid for power, they might have staked their
claims as well as the Europeans.

The only type of sanctions that the Asians could apply in support
of their political claims were moral and economic sanctions. But
these too were very limited in their actual application. Their
economic sanctions resided in the fact that they held in their hands a
fairly substantial proportion of trade and commerce of these
countries. They could, in times of crisis, use these as weapons in
the political struggle. They could, for example, either threaten
to close down their shops or, at worst, pack up their things, including
capital investments, and leave East Africa.

Although a usable form of sanctions, in the absence of a legal
and political apparatus in the background, economic sanctions
have severe limitations and can be used only sparingly. Therefore,
although the Asians were sometimes successful in extracting minor
concessions from the British rulers, this was more because of an
acknowledgement, on the part of the governments, of the Asian
economic power, rather than a consequence of direct application,
or threat of application, of these sanctions by the Asians. In any
case, the Asians had too many stakes and vested interests of their
own in the continuing prosperity of these countries, to want to
create instability through the use of their economic power.

The economic weapon therefore was never sufficiently powerful
for the Asians to stake out large political claims, and this, in an
important way, limited the political ambitions of the community.

The other sort of sanctions that the Asians could apply were
moral sanctions, again neither very reliable nor too readily

applicable. Moral sanctions have meaning only when applied against those who, at least tacitly, accept the validity of the prevailing moral standards. The plea that the reservation of the Kenya Highlands only for the Europeans was a piece of discriminatory legislation which smacked of inequity, was a plea that might have cut some ice with the ordinary Englishmen in the English country-side. On the Europeans in Kenya and for their political mentors in London, with their standards of political morality doctrinally rooted in colonialism, such arguments, of course, would have no effect.

The demands of the Asians in East Africa sometimes were buttressed by the moral support of their erstwhile mother-country, India. But the Indian Government seldom obliged the Asians in East Africa with more than moral support in their fight against the inequities of the Highlands policy or the restricted immigration laws[1]. Generally, the Indian Government, and the Indian people, in their attitude towards their brothers in East Africa showed a complete lack of patience which they often expressed by chiding them, as parents would their naughty children, to behave decently in a foreign land.

This contrasts well with the attitude of most countries towards their nationals abroad: for example, the attitude of the Turkish Government towards the Turks in Cyprus. It was perhaps as well that the Indian Government was reticent in supporting the political demands of the Asians in East Africa, for it brought a sense of realism among the Asians about the limitations of their political manoeuvrability.

The Asians in British Guiana and in Fiji had the backing of numbers to make it worth their while bidding for power on democratic—one man one vote—basis. The Europeans in East Africa could not sustain their power on democratic principles, but had the support of a sanctions machinery resident in London to make possible their continued rule over Africa for more than half a century. The Asians in East Africa had neither the numbers that their brothers in British Guiana and Fiji had, nor the sanctions that their European counterparts in East Africa.

A bid for power was therefore, from the very beginning, a hopeless venture from these two points of view. But there was a third factor also which restrained the Asians from participating in the power-politics of the territories. And this was a realization that even if they were to agitate actively for African independence, the result would be only a change of masters—African masters instead of the British—and not any greater share in the politics of the country.

This might or might not have been borne out by subsequent history, but it was almost universally accepted that the change of masters would not necessarily involve the upgrading of the political status of the Asians.

Whether or not the Asians in East Africa were conscious of the effects of these factors on their political behaviour, it cannot be denied that at the level of meta-politics these were the factors that considerably debilitated the strength of Asian politics. At the level of the Asian masses generally, the popular view was, and still is, that the Asians were primarily traders, not politicians. At the subconscious level they could sense that there were important forces operating which made it highly unlikely that they were going to be anything more than traders. How these, in fact, affected the conduct of Asian political participation, where there was any, in other words, how these affected their political organization and their attitude towards elections, is the problem that we shall now turn to.

The Nature of the Conduct of Asian Politics

The realization that the attainment of political power was beyond the pale of the Asians either under the British or the African rule, and the resigned acceptance of the fact that politically they were the most vulnerable community in East Africa, partly because they had so much vested interests at stake and partly because they lacked any effective and reliable sanctions at their command, these had always exercised a mellowing, almost paralysing, influence not only on the content of Asian politics but also on their political conduct.

First then the manner in which the Asians conducted their small politics. Throughout the British period, the focus of Asian politics had been the individual, brought to limelight either through his own efforts or placed in a position of status by the colonial governments.

There were never existent compelling reasons for the creation of political parties. On the contrary, all the circumstances militated against their creation. There was the official ban on the formation of political parties, much more severely imposed by the British in Kenya during the years of the Mau Mau Emergency than in other parts of East Africa. But even if there were no legal restrictions, there might still have been no Asian political parties. The legal restrictions worried the Africans much more than the Asians. The latter had no strong incentive to form parties, as we know parties in their traditional meaning.

The few times when the Asians did form parties, like the Uganda Action Group (more of a ginger group than a party), and the Kenya Freedom Party, these were formed *ad hoc*, and basically to challenge the existing Asian leadership on some politically controversial issues. As soon as these issues were resolved, these parties dissolved—as we shall see later.

The more normal vehicles of political expression were not parties as we generally know them, but what may variously be called front organizations, associations or congresses. In Kenya there was the Indian National Congress (partaking of the same name as the venerable congress in the mother country); in Uganda there was the Central Council of Indian Association; and in Tanganyika, there was the Asian Association.

The function of these organizations was to act as a two-way channel of communication between the Asians and the governments. The British Government had recognized these organizations since they served a useful function of picking up the Asian leaders for service either in the Legislative Councils or in various government boards and committees.

Although consisting of only a small number of paid-up members, these front organizations purported to represent the entire Asian community, and had their public meetings open to all the members of the community. The result, of course, was that these organizations were always starved of finances. A permanent paid secretary was a luxury that they could indulge in only from time to time depending on the state of their finances. These, quite naturally, had not very wholesome effects on the efficiency of these organizations and therefore on the political health of the community. There was often a lack of communication between the organizations and the public which they purported to represent, with the result that political education of the Asians was hardly their strong merit. This, in turn, merely accentuated the individualistic nature of Asian politics, and explains why there was no serious and consistent practice of discussing political problems at a rational and public level, except when these organizations sporadically arranged public meetings to discuss problems that had arisen *ad hoc*. It is difficult to say, however, how the character of Asian organizations and the nature of their politics could have been otherwise, since, except for a few ambitious individuals, politics was not a paying proposition for the community as a whole, for reasons that we have already seen above.

Another effect of weak political organization of the Asians

that may be mentioned in passing is the consistently bad press they had both during the British period and after. The Asians were often painted in most unkind terms, for example, as exploiters and collaborators of the British, and although there is some degree of truth in this, as there always is in all forms of political mud-slinging, the Asian organizations hardly ever made serious attempts to rebut these allegations, except again, intermittently and on an individual basis.

The weakness of the Asian organizations was not only at the level of each territory, but also at the interterritorial level. There was almost daily contact between individual Asian businessmen in the three countries, and to some extent there must also have been an exchange of views over the common problems of the Asians in East Africa, but such contacts as existed were never institutiona-lized with the result that not only was there no interterritorial support for each others' political demands, but there was also complete lack of a system of mutual advice on each others' problems. Such lessons as were learnt by the Asians in one country from the experiences of their brothers in another country were purely incidental, *ad hoc*, and uninstitutionalized. Thus the Kenya Freedom Party which was created in February 1960, although not consciously modelled on the Uganda Action Group set up at the beginning of 1959, yet had common features with it both in respect of the circumstances in which they were created and in the policies that they adopted. It was difficult not to learn from the experiences of the brothers over the boundaries, but the lessons were learnt casually rather than through a concerted effort. In general, however, Kenya set the pace in determining the general mood of the Asians in the three territories, partly because there was always so much more happening in Kenya than in Tanganyika or Uganda, and partly because Nairobi was so much more Asian than either Kampala or Dar es Salaam. After 1958, however, the roles were reversed because of the faster political development in Tanganyika and Uganda. Kenya lagged behind, giving an opportunity to the Asians in Kenya to learn from the experiences of their brothers in Tanganyika and Uganda.

Since there existed no traditional type of political parties among the Asians except for short periods in Kenya and Uganda, and since Asian organizations in the political sphere were very weak, the task of getting elected as members of the Legislative Council or the Executive Council in the British days was very much dependent on the efforts of the individuals who aspired for such public office.

This, of course, meant that only the more rich among the Asians could afford to join politics and contest elections, or those who had either good communal support or rich friends to finance electioneering campaigns.

Communal voting was at once the inevitable outcome of individualistic politics and the scourge of Asian politics in East Africa. That the candidates should emphasize communal, religious and language differences among their Asian voters so as to muster support for themselves, is, however, not a new phenomenon, and had a parallel, with their African counterparts who incited tribalism to win votes. The only difference was that from the national point of view, Asian politics were insignificant anyway, so that communalism among them made little or no difference to the national politics, as did tribalism.

But as far as the Asians were concerned the effects of communalism were not always healthy. The British Government quite effectively used communal differences, whenever they felt that the Asians acting as a group would prove a nuisance, if not a positive obstruction to legislation. This therefore sapped whatever little political strength that the Asians had.

Worse still, the communal voting and communal seats in the Legislative Council were fissiparous in their effects on the already weak Asian organizations. Thus when British India was partitioned into India and Pakistan in 1947, the Muslim Asians in East Africa demanded the partitioning of Asian organizations. They thus created their own organizations, like the Central Council of Moslem Association in Uganda and demanded separate seats in the Legislative Council. There was nothing very surprising about this development, since in any elections carried on communal basis, it was only a realistic assumption that the Muslim Asians would inevitably be outvoted by their Hindu rivals. The communal phenomenon had its more serious, and tragic (for the Asians) implications in the at least theoretical possibility that all the 'minorities' among the Asians should strike out for a claim of 'self-determination' and demand to be separately represented in the Legislative Councils. As far as the Sikhs of Kenya are concerned the issue had in fact gone at one time beyond mere theoretical possibility. The actual creation of a separate seat for the Sikhs happily did not materialize.

Communal representation plagued Kenya Asian politics more than it did Tanganyika and Uganda. Kenya had always been a hotbed of rival racial, tribal and communal factions, and the British Government cannot be credited with making even a minimum of effort to discourage these fissiparous tendencies. Theirs was a realistic policy of playing one faction against another—this is true even if it has now become a cliché. The British colonial policy of divide and rule was an extension of, and perhaps only another name for, her traditional policy of balance of power in Europe. Just as it served the British interests best when there existed a balance or an equilibrium of power among the different nations in Europe, so a balance of power between the different races, tribes and communities in the colonies served her interests best. In Europe, Britain traditionally supported the weaker nation against the stronger (Belgium in preference to Germany, for instance); similarly, in the colonies, British policy was to support the weaker faction against the stronger: the small tribes in the small tribe-big tribe conflict, the Muslims in the Hindu-Muslim conflict, and so on right down the line.

In Uganda and in Tanganyika where communal divisions were not so pronounced or so much played up by the colonial government, as in Kenya, the Asians resisted being represented in the Legislative Councils on strictly communal basis. This did not, however, prevent voting on communal lines during the time of elections. Among other effects of communal voting there are two that are worth mentioning. First, with the exception of a few, the people who were supposed to be representing the Asian opinion in the governing councils of the three territories were elected not necessarily for their policies, but more often for their communal popularity.[2] The second effect, and a corollary of the first, was that although there were always elements within the Asian communities who were much more radical in their political thinking than the rest of their people, they could not gain a voice in the governing bodies for lack of communal support, either because they belonged to small communal groups, or because their support was scattered over different communal groups without having a full support of one large community to enable them to win elections.

It was against this background that the Asians faced the challenge of African nationalism to which we shall now turn.

African Nationalism and the Asian Response

Nationalism for the Asians was not a new experience. Many of them had known it in the 1920s and 1930s and even as recently as in the 1940s. It was until recently customary for the Asians in East Africa to celebrate the anniversary of the independence of India and Pakistan. Although they were so far from their countries of origin, the independence of India and Pakistan was an emotional reality for them, in the celebration of which they could not but help participate. While this was an understandable human reaction to the success of a freedom movement in which they were emotionally involved, it was a reaction which stopped at the coasts of India. The emotion of freedom and the sentiment of anti-colonialism were not, except in the case of a few individuals, operative in the context of East Africa. Why?

In retrospect it would seem that if the Asians in East Africa had shown the same amount of exuberance for freedom, and if they had completely identified with the African aspirations, and still more if they had taken the initiative to start the struggle against colonialism even when the Africans were not ready themselves, then the Asians might have reserved for themselves a position of respect and leadership among the Africans today.

Now why did not the Asians transplant in the East African soil their spirit of anti-colonialism which they had experienced much before the Africans? Various explanations can be given for this, ranging from the most sinister plots to the most palpable excuses. The truth may lie somewhere in between.

One explanation, with some degree of truth, may be that the Asian immigrant in East Africa was a different kind of person from his brother back in India. Incidentally a similar observation is made of the Englishman too: the Englishman in a colonial situation was a different kind of creature—almost Fascist—from the Englishman back at home—liberal, humanitarian. The Asians in East Africa were a trading community who came here primarily to improve their economic fortunes. They could, therefore, be pictured in the most sinister terms: a hypocritical people who opposed the British régime in India but favoured it in East Africa so they might continue to enjoy economic prosperity.

Put in this way, it seems an ugly truth, if rather simplified. There was, however, an obvious dichotomy between what the bulk of the Asians felt in their hearts about African nationalism, and the public stand that their leaders had taken, both in their actions and in their pronouncements. In their public pronouncements, the Asian leaders in all the three territories had, except in a few isolated cases, from the very beginning taken a positive stand in favour of constitutional development towards self-government based on adult universal suffrage and a common roll. In other words, the Asian leaders had envisaged independence under African majorities as the ultimate goal to aspire towards in the three territories—even in Kenya. Thus as far back as 15 February, 1946, the president of the Kenya Indian Association in outlining the 'aims of Indians in Kenya' had strongly opposed any attempt by the British Government prematurely to give self-government to Kenya under the existing European majority in the Legislative Council, in the same way as today the African states are opposed to a premature independence to Southern Rhodesia under white supremacy. The president had then warned that if the Labour government were to succumb to the threat of non-constitutional assumption of power by the Kenya Europeans, then the Indians would have no alternative but to bring all non-European races on to a common platform and advise some common action.

In the same vein, the Asian leaders, in their public pronouncements, favoured the representation of the Africans by the Africans themselves in the Legislative Councils at a time when they were represented by unofficial Europeans; they almost invariably supported the African demand for increased representation in the Legislative Councils; and they fought for the principle of equality for the races, including, for instance, the opening of the White Highlands for the Asians and the Africans as well as for the Europeans, and the ending of racial segregation in public places.

There can be no doubt that even when privately the Asians had reservations about the ability of the Africans to rule themselves, they were sincere about their public stand, and were influenced partly by ideological considerations of equity and justice, partly by a realistic consideration that power must eventually pass into the hands of the Africans, and partly because their own countries of origin, particularly India, had taken an open stand against the continuance of colonialism as an important objective of their foreign policies, and were exerting their diplomatic influence to this end through organizations like the United Nations and the Commonwealth.

But there is also no doubt that, excepting again a few individuals, the bulk of the Asians were ambivalent in their attitude towards the rising force of African nationalism. In public, it was necessary for the leaders to accept the inevitable and call it virtue; in private, one could indulge in the sin of thinking at variance with African nationalism. What follows is a possible explanation for this attitude, not a justification for it.

Fear is a natural reaction of human beings against the unknown. This is doubly so for a man with vested interests which might be threatened by the unknown events. In retrospect, the Asians would

perhaps seem to have been unduly pessimistic, but fear was none-
theless a dominant characteristic of the Asians in the 1950s.
Why did they then continue to invest money in business in the
1950s? The answer must be that the Asians expected the British
rule to continue for several more decades. In this they were in good
company; the United Nations Mission which visited Tanganyika
in the fifties reckoned that it would be a couple of decades before
the country was ready for independence. However, once their
expectations were proved false, the Asians were quick to send their
capital abroad.

Now why were the Asians dominated by a sense of fear, rather
than optimism as they should have been at the prospect of independence? Again there could be various explanations, ranging from the
one that the Asians were merely birds of passage who were beginning
to see the end of their season in East Africa and must face the unpleasant task of returning to their homelands or finding new grounds,
to the explanation that the Asians did not understand the nature
of African nationalism because of a failure of emotional communication between the Asian and the African leaders. There is some
element of truth in all this, but one cannot get away from two
basic sociological facts that were at the root of such fears: one
was that the Asians were a separate economic class with vested
interests; and the second that they constituted a minority immigrant
community which could easily be identified as belonging to a
different race altogether. It was as if two revolutions—economic
and racial—were springing a surprise at the Asians who happened
to be at the other end of the stick. And there hardly existed any
mitigating factors: visibly there existed almost no strong African
group whose interest could be identified with the Asians. Furthermore, events moved so fast that the Asians—conservative in their
ways in any event—could not adjust themselves quickly so as to
identify themselves with African nationalism absolutely.

African nationalism was therefore black African nationalism,
even though there were individual Asians who were genuinely in
basic sympathy with the African aspirations. Self-determination
was known and seen in racial terms by the Africans and not in purely
national terms.

African nationalists had shouted for self-governments, not
necessarily good governments—self-rule was decidedly purported
to be better than foreign rule. The majority of the Asians had
accepted the idea of self-government for the Africans, but they
were also concerned that there should be good government, good

in their ability to maintain law and order while they continued with their business. The British Government at least provided them with that. Chances were that the African governments might not, since theirs was not a task to uphold the *status quo* but to change it. Existing evidence did not, in any case, inspire them with any degree of confidence in African governments: the Asian shops were first to be looted even if the dispute was between the Europeans and the Africans or among the Africans themselves. And finally, when independence was to come, power was to be transferred to the Africans, and this was also recognized by the Asian leaders. So it was a question of exchanging one master for the other, and who was to say whether the new master might not turn out to be even more difficult?

It is in this atmosphere of fear and scepticism about the future that the response of the Asians to the challenge of African nationalism must be assessed. Concerned, as they were, with the problem of security in a future East Africa, the Asians began to look around for electioneering and constitutional safeguards. Communal roll, reserved seats for the Asians in the national assemblies, and even at times qualified franchise based on education or property, and the institution of a Bill of Rights in the constitutions became common vocabulary among the Asians during this time.

In Tanganyika, the first response of the Asians to the 1954-58 British idea of creating a multi-racial society based on an equality between the races, was to accept it as the most sanguine solution to their future problems. The Asians, for a time, deluded themselves into thinking that they could share power on a basis of equality with the Europeans and the Africans in Tanganyika. Under the leadership of a few farsighted individuals, it later dawned on them that such a formula was not practicable. If Tanganyika was to achieve independence at all, and to break her links with the sanctions machinery in London, a system based on power shared on a tripartite basis could not form a lasting settlement of the problem of the three races in Tanganyika. Besides, it was palpably unfair that the Asians with only about $1\frac{1}{2}$ per cent of the population and the Europeans with still less should share out two thirds of the seats in a national assembly, leaving only one third for the remaining 98 per cent of the population.

The emergence of TANU under the wise leadership of Mwalimu Julius Nyerere made it easier for the Asians to opt out finally in favour of completely identifying themselves politically with the Africans. Although the 1958-59 elections for the Legislative Council were based on the idea of equal representation between the races (one African, one European and one Asian member from each of the ten constituencies), and although elections took place on a limited franchise, the institution of common roll at that early stage brought victory to either the African members of the TANU or to independent European and Asian candidates who enjoyed its formal support. At the September 1960 general elections the idea of equal representation for the three races was finally abandoned, although out of 71 seats, 11 seats were still reserved for the Asians and 10 for the Europeans. Again, on a common roll, but with a widened franchise, 70 of the 71 seats were won by the TANU and the TANU-supported independent candidates.

In Uganda and in Kenya too, the Asian leaders for a time toyed with the idea of electioneering safeguards for their future, namely communal roll and reserved seats in the national assemblies. In both countries the problem sparked a lively controversy and a split in the existing Asian leadership.

In Uganda, it led to the creation of a ginger group called the Uganda Action Group in the beginning of 1959. Its avowed policies were to challenge what its members called the 'old guard' Asian leadership, and to bring about a political rethinking of the issues currently at controversy, and to attempt to get Indians admitted to the African political parties. The leadership of the UAG consisted mostly of young radical thinkers among the Asians who, partly because of their experiences in the U.K. from where they could view events in Uganda with a healthy perspective and partly because of a streak of genuine idealism in support of African demands, vigorously came out against communal voting roll and reserved minority seats for safeguarding the interests of the Asians. They realized it much faster than the old leadership that such safeguards had no value unless sufficient goodwill was built up between the Asian minority and the African majority. A few Asian seats in the National Assembly voted on a communal roll would have permanently placed a thorn among the African majorities, and in the end was not good for the Asians as well.

In Kenya the split among the Asian leadership took place at a much more dramatic moment, namely, during the eve of the 1960 Lancaster House Conference. The main points of difference again seemed to be on the question of whether to support the African nationalists unqualifiedly, or whether to demand electioneering safeguards for the minorities by retaining communal rolls and reserved seats for the minorities in the National Assembly. The more radical members of the Indian National Congress formed a splinter group called the Kenya Freedom Party in February, 1960, ostensibly with membership open to all races, but really an Indian political party designed, like the Uganda Action Group, to challenge the more conservative stand taken by the Asian representatives in the organs of the government (and also at the Lancaster Conference), and to attempt to get Asians admitted as members of African political parties. Like the UAG the KFP also stood out in favour of 'independence now' rather than independence by gradual stages, a common roll instead of a communal roll, and 'open seats' rather than reserved seats for the minorities. It is difficult to ascertain how far the Asian public was divided as between the conservative and cautious stand taken by the Indian National Congress and the radical stand taken by the KFP, since the elections in 1960-61, like all previous elections, were influenced by considerations of communalism.

The Lancaster House Conference unmistakably altered the course of events in Kenya: the inevitability of African independence was brought much closer to reality than many people had thought possible. It also instituted common roll instead of communal roll; the position of the minority communities was safeguarded by the reservation of 20 of the 53 seats—10 Europeans, 8 Asians and 2 Arabs—to be filled in by primary elections within their respective communities. In addition, provision was made for constitutional safeguards of human rights and rights over property.

Both the UAG and the KFP were thus short-lived phenomena which had sprung up *ad hoc* at a crisis period, and were dissolved after their aims were achieved. While it lasted the KFP functioned more like a party than the UAG and actually contested the 1960-61 elections against its time-honoured adversary, the Indian National Congress[3]. At the time of their formal dissolution, the leaders of UAG and KFP made a similar statement to the effect that there was no longer any reason for their parties to continue to exist since they could now directly become members of the African nationalist political parties.

Asian Politics in an Independent East Africa

The incidence of independence has fundamentally transformed the character of Asian politics in East Africa, both in its content and its conduct. Independence has not meant simply a change of masters, as was widely believed before. With independence have come important qualitative changes in the nature of Asian politics owing essentially to two factors. The first of these factors is ideological.

The principal difference between the ideology of the colonial governments and that of the present African governments is their attitudes towards racialism. The British colonial policy hinged on racial separatism which divided the three principal races not only on a cultural and social plane, but also on an economic and political basis: the Europeans occupied the apex of the triangle; the Africans formed the base; and the Asians occupied the middle. The present governments of Kenya, Uganda and Tanzania are determined to roll back the policy of racial separatism. The Europeans could sustain their rule only by maintaining the myth of their racial superiority; the Africans do not necessarily have to assert the myth of African superiority because they have the advantage of numbers that the Europeans did not have. The British interests in the colonies were best served by a policy of divide and rule as between different races and different tribes; the present governments believe that their interests would best be served by forging national unity between their people, whatever their racial origins or tribal backgrounds. The British had thus instituted separate representation for the three races in the organs of government; the independent governments of East Africa have deprecated political representation on racial lines. This has, in principle, met the approval of the Asians, as we saw above.

This then is the first significant change that has come about since independence. The second important change has been in the direction of the nationalization of citizenship. Since *uhuru*, most of the Africans almost automatically ceased to hold British passports and opted out for the citizenship of their respective countries. The minority races, and significantly the Asians, were offered very generous terms for the acquisition of the new citizenships as well. That the terms are generous can hardly be disputed if one were to compare the citizenship laws of East Africa with those of, for instance, Ceylon and Burma where large Indian minorities reside. This magnanimous attitude on the part of the East African governments may be accounted for by the fact that the citizenship laws came as a package deal along with independence. But the generous citizenship laws might in part be a reflection of the recognition paid to the role of the Asians in the future economic development of independent East Africa, and in part a reflection of a genuine streak of charitableness felt by the African leaders towards a small minority race. The point about the recognition of the role of the Asians in the future economic development of the countries is mentioned particularly to explode the myth often held by minority immigrant races that they have a right to enjoy equal status in the countries of their adoption because they 'built up' these countries. This argument unfortunately reeks of the same odour as when the Europeans in pre-independent Algeria claimed the right to stay because they 'built' Algeria. Such arguments make no impact in politics. In so far as African leaders tend to play down the past contribution of the Asians in the economic development of East Africa, it is evident that their offer of equal rights of citizenship is based on the contribution they are expected to make in the future rather than as a reward for their past work.

Before we work out the impact of these political-constitutional changes on Asian politics, it may be mentioned, in passing, that the offer of equal rights as citizens to the Asians in East Africa was not effected without a certain amount of opposition from quarters who felt that the Asians did not deserve much generosity. In Tanganyika, for instance, in the months immediately following independence, there was considerable hostility, even at the parliamentary level, to permitting the Asians to sit in parliament and to enrol as members of the TANU. The reasons for such hostility are understandable not only at the emotional level—it is not easy to be equanimous with an immigrant minority race that has, rightly or wrongly, been stigmatized as having exploited the indigenous people but also at the level of strict logicality—to accord equal rights as between two obviously (economically) unequal communities is palpably to lay legal foundations for perpetuating that inequality. Demands based on equity and justice have more often been the weapon of the under-privileged. In East Africa, the concept of equal treatment could well become the tool of the privileged to perpetuate their privileges. The role of the new independent governments in the popular eyes was first to remove the existing inequalities before talking about equality. It is a tribute to African leadership, particularly of Tanganyika whose cue the others followed, that the public passion in this regard was effectively controlled. The leaders who achieved independence for their own countries by raising the banner of equality and human rights could not see them denied to a foreign minority who came in their midst by an historical accident. Although in later years, practice, specially with regard to Africanization and promotion in the civil service, did not always conform to the law of equal treatment, one needs a little more thinking to realize that this discrepancy between law and administration is really a case of law based on a doctrinal foundation of equality bending down under the weight of the hard realities of life. From the Asian point of view, it is better that there should exist some disparity between theory and practice, than that inequality as between races should become part of the law of the land. If it is an evil, it is at least the lesser of the two evils.

The distinction between theory and practice may be utilized again to work out the impact of independence on the nature of Asian politics in East Africa. In theory, almost all the Asians could have opted to take up the citizenships of one of the three countries in the two years of grace period given to them after independence. (In Kenya this period has not yet expired). In theory again there is nothing to prevent the Asians from joining national political parties, and from contesting elections both at the level of central government and at the municipal or regional levels. In theory, indeed, there is no reason why an Asian may not become a president or a prime minister of one of the countries. Theoretically the Asians therefore enjoy a right that was not even open to them during the British rule.

Both in theory and in practice there is no place for the Asian community as a distinct political entity in East African politics, since there is no more representation on racial lines. The Asian member in the former Legislative Council, even if elected on a communal vote, was deemed to represent the 'voice of the Asians'. The Asian member of parliament today cannot have such pretensions, for he is deemed, in a broad sense, to represent the nation, and in a narrow sense, the interests of his political party. In practice, therefore, an Asian aspiring to play a part in parliamentary politics must seek support from a political party, for there are few seats, even in the urban areas, which can be won through Asian communal support only. A successful Asian politician today is correspondingly different from his predecessor in the British period. He is likely to be more radical in his political views, and is likely to sing the song of African socialism and to shout '*Harambee!*' a little louder than the rest, or else he may not be noticed. As for the old Asian institutions like the Kenya Indian National Congress or the Uganda Central Council of Indian Association, they do not seem to have been significantly affected by independence. Of course, they have re-oriented their policies in the direction of the wind of change, but their leadership has still remained largely in the old hands, and their function not very different from before, namely, that of acting as an informal two way channel of communication between the government and the Asians, and as a forum for sounding opinions on the problems of Asians in East Africa.

For the large majority of Asians this is a period of agonising adjustments to political changes that have come with the speed of a hurricane. A good number of these have not taken up local citizenship either because they are pessimistic about their future in East Africa, or because they are optimistic about their prospects in the outside world. Like pious men who, if they try hard can find evidence everywhere to substantiate their theory that sin in the world is on the increase, those among the Asians who are pessimistic about the future can also find evidence to confirm their worst fears. This evidence may relate to events in one of the sister countries (like the looting of Indian shops during the Zanzibar *coup d'etat* and the Tanganyika army mutiny in 1964), or to instances of alleged discrimination against Asians, particularly those in the civil services, and specially when the alleged victims had taken up local citizenship. They are convinced that taking up citizenship would not alter the fact that the Asians could aspire to no more than second class citizenship. It is difficult to persuade them that the governments have to 'Africanize' (in racial terms) both the economy as well as the administration in order to correct the 'racial imbalance' created as a result of deliberate British colonial policy, which the Asians largely tolerated, if not actually endorsed. Perhaps it is an understandable reaction on the part of the Asians: it is difficult to digest rational arguments when one's promotion, perhaps even the payroll, is threatened by an allegedly discriminatory action of the government. But since correcting the imbalance is essentially a short-term objective, there is still time to prove to the pessimistic brand of Asians that their fears were misplaced. If, however, the policy of Africanization interpreted in racial terms becomes a long-term policy, a persistent phenomenon, then the more optimistic among the Asians are likely to get disillusioned as well.

There are several economic consequences of the decision by a percentage of the Asians (what percentage cannot as yet be ascertained) not to take up local citizenship. However, what we are concerned with here are the political consequences. Briefly these are: firstly, political disenfranchisement of these Asians with the result that the base of Asian voters is much smaller than their visible presence in the urban areas might indicate—this has driven an aspiring Asian politician much more in the hands of African voters; secondly, the split among the Asian minority community as between citizens and non-citizens with the result that not only has this debilitated the political strength of the Asian community, *qua* community, but it has also set up a situation in which those who have acquired citizenship are now asking for preferential treatment as against their non-citizen brothers (for example, on the question of the issue of trading licences); thirdly, the creation of a situation by which, since a large section of the Asians have retained British citizenship, the British Government has to meet their international legal and moral obligations towards the protection of lives and alien rights of nationals of a distinctly different race; and finally, since the non-acquisition of citizenship is taken to be symbolic of the Asian distrust of African governments, the acerbation of racial tension between the Asians and the Africans, with the result that old accusations are given fresh blood.

For those who have acquired East African citizenship, the problem of adjustment demands immediate attention. Among these, a great number of people, particularly the older generation, are still emotionally ill-equipped to reconcile themselves to the changed situation, although intellectually they are prepared to integrate in the present African societies. Integration, whatever form it takes, would of necessity involve a gradual whittling down of Asian ethnocentricism, and their isolationist group mentality, enforced during the British rule, of maintaining a closed society of language, religion and Old World customs and social values. This is not going to be easy, for the process may involve not only an attack on the Asians' vested interests, but possibly a breaking down of their whole framework of reference.

The extent to which the Asians will integrate in East Africa and cease to be identified as 'a problem' will largely depend on the activities of the Asians themselves. But it will also depend on the lead provided by the African majorities. The differences between the Asians and the Africans may lessen by the emergence of common social and economic interests. But whether the convergence of interests (for example, trade union interests) will result in co-operation or heightened competition and tension remains to be seen. The instrumental factor here would be the attitude of the African majorities towards the racial minority. Thinking with the race, as the Nazi thinking with blood, may sometimes prove stronger than thinking in terms of economic class. In the United States, for instance, racial prejudice in the form of 'lily-white unionism' has proved stronger than the Marxist myth of class solidarity. Here therefore one needs to ask how African socialism would be defined, and what place a racial minority would have in it. It is obvious that if the term is defined purely in racial terms, then the Asian community in East Africa would for ever be alienated, since it is not easy to change one's racial pigment. Then the Asian 'problem' would continue to persist, almost by definition. If there is some accommodation for the Asians in African socialism, as indeed the thinking of present African leaders indicates, then it would considerably facilitate the eventual integration of the meagre 2 per cent Asian minority in the tasks of nation-building. And the task of nation-building involves for the Asians not only their traditional functions of saving and capital accumulation for economic development, but also and importantly, helping the governments of the three countries to fill the historical gap of racial imbalance left since the colonial days. The Asians must co-operate, for instance, in credit societies, co-operative schemes and so on, and must open up their businesses to participation by the Africans. They must, in other words, consciously and actively break all forms of racial barriers even if admittedly this is easier said than done. More cannot be recommended for the subject falls out of the scope of this paper.

Conclusion

In concluding this paper let us briefly address ourselves to three evaluative questions. First: how much credit should the Asians deserve for the ultimate independence of Kenya, Uganda and Tanzania? The answer, from what we have observed above, must be: very little. And it could not have been otherwise. The Asians had little or no sanctions even to support their demands for equality with the Europeans—any premature agitation for independence on their part might not only have fallen through but possibly even been misunderstood. Demands for independence became politically consequential only when the Africans made them. The Asians might have joined the freedom movement much more actively than they actually did, for although officially the Asians consistently favoured constitutional progress towards self-government, they were not nearly as radical as their African brothers, and the great majority of them had mental reservations about independence that must have neutralized the impact of their public policy. There were, of course, some who did in fact whole-heartedly join with the Africans, but these were few and far between. In any event, the credit for the independence of East Africa must unmistakably go to the African freedom movements, and, what is often not realized, to the wind of change that swept the continent following the Second World War.

The second question we may ask ourselves is: how much were the Asians an obstruction in the march towards independence? Again the answer must be: very little. It was not so much the case of the Asians determining or even influencing the pace towards independence, as the fact of oncoming independence influencing Asian behaviour. The Asians were no more than a straw in the political wind: they were not so much blowing the wind, as were being blown about. It is true that there were some reactionaries among the Asians, but they were for a large part ineffectual. It is also true that the presence of an Asian minority had introduced tricky constitutional problems—on the question of, for instance, reserved seats, or the controversy between common roll and communal roll—but these problems were more a worry of the Asians themselves, rather than of the whole country. They had to adjust themselves to the situation of impending independence, and how best to do it was their problem.

Finally, the question: what impact are the Asians likely to make on the politics of East Africa in future? The answer is about the same: hardly any. Politically, they are impotent. This does not mean that there will not be political consequences of the fact that they still largely control the distributive side of the economy, and that they constitute an easily identifiable and relatively prosperous racial minority. What it means is that, as a community, they cannot influence the nature of the régimes that will come into power, and the kind of political-constitutional changes that may come about in East Africa. They would do well to face this reality, and to identify themselves with African aspirations, for these are very reasonable aspirations in the context of modern international relations.

References

1. The Indian Government, for instance, seldom took up matters on a diplomatic level, so that the influence of India in East Africa was much less after her independence than before, for at least before, the British Raj in India was a little sensitive to the effects British laws in East Africa might have on the sentiments of their subject-race in India, e.g., on the question of immigration.

2. George Bennett and Carl Rosberg in their book *The Kenyatta Elections, Kenya, 1960-1961* (O.U.P., 1961) give a good account of Asian communal elections in Kenya. See specially p. 115-116 where they write: 'However much leaders may proclaim that it must and should end, all Asian elections in Kenya in the past . . . have been dominated by communalism. The first document noticed on many an Asian candidate's desk, and the first subject of conversation with the agent of any candidate, was the breakdown of the voters' roll by communities . . . . It always remained remarkable how Asian candidates carried the exact figures of voters of each community in their head so that they could, often most accurately, foretell the results.'

3. Although members of KFP stood in the elections as 'independents' rather than on any party 'tickets.'

4. An Economic Survey

Dharam P. Ghai

An attempt is made in this chapter to describe the main patterns of economic activity of the Asians settled in the three East African countries. This attempt seems worth making not only because of the intrinsic importance of the subject itself but also for the light it may throw on other facets of the life of Asians in East Africa. However, any such attempt is severely restricted by the lack of adequate data on the role of Asians in the East African economies. What follows, therefore, is no more than a rough sketch of the dominant patterns of economic activity of East African Asians, built up from bits and pieces of available data[1] and supplemented by qualitative observations.

The first step in this economic survey must be an assessment of the size, structure and growth of Asian population in East Africa. The census reports show that the Asian population in the three countries increased from 183,800 in 1948 to an estimated 352,300 in 1963, an increase of over 90 per cent in 15 years. This increase is of course the result of both a natural increase in population and a considerable net immigration into East Africa. Unfortunately, we do not have adequate information to separate out the effects of these two sources of population growth. Some very rough estimates made by the writer indicate that as much as 60 per cent of the population increase may have been due to immigration alone. It is, however, noteworthy that there has been a steady decline in net immigration into East Africa since the mid-fifties when it was running at an annual average of 10,000 persons. In contrast to this, the 1962 figures show that new permanent immigration of Asians into East Africa was almost exactly offset by permanent emigration from these countries; while the figures for the first quarter of 1964 in Kenya show that the permanent Asian emigration was almost double the Asian immigration.

It is not intended here to offer an explanation of this pattern of migration nor to speculate on the future trends in migration. The subsequent sections will deal with the employment opportunities for Asians in East Africa and will thus offer a partial explanation of the above trends in migration. Suffice it to say here that the slowing down in the rate of growth of the East African economies in recent years and the increasing difficulties in the way of Asian immigration have combined to bring net immigration to a trickle. It seems that for some time to come the main source of the expansion of the Asian population will be internal. Estimates of the natural growth rate of the Asian population vary between 2.5 and 3 per cent per annum. There are, however, strong indications of a gradual decline in the rate of population growth, caused mainly by a decline in birth-rates. It would be a safe assumption to make that the natural rate of growth of the Asian population is unlikely to exceed 2.5 per cent per annum in future.

Even more important from an economic point of view is the structure of the current Asian population. Despite a substantial inflow of Asian immigrants in the past, the general shape of the age-distribution of this population has tended increasingly to approximate rapidly expanding and locally born population with high fertility and declining mortality rates. The result is that the population 'pyramid' has a broad base and a very slender apex. Typically, about 42 per cent of the entire population consists of persons in the 0-14 years age-groups, with over 54 per cent in the 15-59 years age-group and slightly over 3 per cent in the 60 and over age-group. This is in marked contrast to the age-structure to be found in countries experiencing a slower rate of population increase, which have a higher proportion in the working-age groups. The effect of this pattern of population 'pyramid' of Asians in East Africa is to impose a heavy burden on the 'productive' section of the population for the sustenance of a relatively larger proportion of 'dependents'.

We are further interested in the geographical distribution of the Asian population in East Africa. Of the total Asian population of 352,300 in 1963 in the three mainland territories, more than 50 per cent or 180,000 reside in Kenya; while the Asian population of Uganda and Tanganyika is estimated at 82,100 and 90,200 respectively. Of this population, about 60 to 65 per cent were born in East Africa, the rest immigrated from India and Pakistan. It may be of interest to notice that the Asian population represents 1.3 per cent of the total population of East Africa. An important characteristic of this population is its high degree of urbanization. In 1957, no less than 75 per cent of the total Asian population in Tanganyika lived in 14 townships and 60 per cent in the five largest towns.

Similarly, in 1959, 75 per cent of the Asian population in Uganda was reported to be living in urban areas. This proportion is likely to be even higher now because of a marked drift of the Asian population towards larger towns and cities all over East Africa in recent years. The 1962 census in Kenya reveals the extent of this drift: no fewer than 85 per cent of the Asian population in Kenya was reported to be living in the five largest towns. There are more Asians living in Nairobi alone than in the whole of Uganda or Tanganyika. The urbanized pattern of Asian settlement in East Africa is in marked contrast to the pattern established in other countries where Indians have settled in considerable numbers such as British Guiana, West Indies, Fiji Islands and to a lesser extent, South Africa. It will be shown later than the urban pattern of Asian settlement in East Africa was partly due to the several economic restrictions placed on the members of the Asian community. Meanwhile, it is important to note the far-reaching political, economic and social consequences of the concentration of Asian population in urban areas. It is this factor which has been responsible for the 'Indian look' of almost all the major towns and cities in East Africa. Furthermore, it has facilitated the organization of the Asian community into a number of tight, closely-knit communal groups and hence increased its isolation from other races. Economically, it has reduced the dependence of the community on other races. The fact that many businessmen, lawyers, doctors, accountants and other professional men derive a large proportion of their earnings from the Asian clientéle, further reinforces their natural propensity to look to the Asian community for all their needs and aspirations.

A description and evaluation of the Asian role in the East African economies can only be made in qualitative terms at the present stage. However, in order to put our subsequent discussion in proper perspective, it is necessary to give a few statistics about the number and industrial distribution of the economically active[2] section of the Asian population. The census reports indicate that the economically active population constituted about 25-27 per cent of the entire Asian population in the three East African countries. This is a much lower proportion than among the European community; the main reasons for this are, of course, the higher proportion of European women in employment, as well as a lower proportion of children and retired persons in the European population of East Africa. Another remarkable feature of the Asian community, again in sharp contrast to the European, is the relatively small proportion of the economically active population working as employees. However, the territorial patterns in this respect are sufficiently divergent for us to consider each country separately.

In 1962, Kenya had the largest class of wage and salary earners, who at 36,100 constituted a little less than 70 per cent of the economically active population of the Asian community. At the other extreme is Uganda, where the corresponding figure for employees is only 9,900 persons, about 45 per cent of the economically active population. Tanganyika is somewhere in the middle with 12,100 employees, about 50 per cent of the economically active population. The rest of the economically active population is made up of employers, own-account workers and unemployed. The higher proportion of employees in Kenya is in part due to the advanced state of the economy, but mainly due to the substantially larger number of persons employed by the public sector. In Kenya, public sector provided employment to 33 per cent of the total Asian employees in 1962; the corresponding figures for Tanganyika and Uganda are 25 per cent and 18 per cent. The importance of the public sector in Kenya is mainly, though not wholly, due to the location of the headquarters of all the EACSO services in Nairobi; very nearly 40 per cent of the employees in the Kenya public sector work for the Railways and Harbours, Posts and Telecommunications and the Common Services Organization.

We have far more detailed information on the industrial distribution and income levels of Asian employees than of the self-employed and employers. However, before we come to a detailed analysis of employees, it is necessary to say something about the broad industrial classification of the entire Asian population of working age. A study of the various census reports shows that there is considerable similarity between the pattern of industrial distribution of the Asian economically active population in Uganda and Tanganyika. Broadly speaking, between 45 to 50 per cent of the total Asian working population in both these countries derive their livelihood from commerce, defined to include wholesale and retail trade, banking and insurance. Manufacturing and public services each account for a further 10 per cent of the working population. In Tanganyika, transport and communications, and in Uganda agriculture, including cotton ginning and coffee curing, are the next important category, accounting for about 9 per cent of the working population in each country. The rest of the population derive their livelihood from the provision of various services, from construction, etc. The pattern in Kenya differs somewhat, mainly because a much higher proportion of the working population are dependent on employment for their earnings. Consequently, we find that commerce is relatively less important as a source of livelihood, while public services, transport and communications, manufacturing and miscellaneous services are more important.

The great importance of commerce as a source of income for Asians in East Africa is clearly brought out by the above figures. However, some readers will be surprised to find that the contribution of commerce is not greater still, for Asians in East Africa are often described as a 'race of shopkeepers.' Next in importance are public services, manufacturing, transport and communications, and miscellaneous services. Agriculture is perhaps the only major industry in East Africa where Asian participation has been relatively unimportant.

We can now turn to a detailed analysis of the Asian employees in East Africa. The official statistics show that there was a steady increase in the number of Asian employees throughout the post-war period until 1960, but that the numbers employed have been falling in the last four years. This fall in employment has been general and not confined to Asians alone, and is a reflection of a considerable slowing down in the expansion of the East African economies in recent years. The impact of Africanization of public services and the economy did not make itself felt until 1963; its effect on the employment opportunities for Asians will be discussed in a subsequent section. Here we may notice another important development in the Asian labour market in the post-war period: a steady relative increase in the importance of female employees. In Kenya the number of Asian female employees has gone up from just over 600 in 1948 to 3,750 in 1962, while the number of total Asian employees has risen by a little over 60 per cent during the same period. We find a similar, though not such dramatic, trend in other parts of East Africa. In 1962, females constituted about 10 per cent of the total Asian labour force in East Africa. As might be expected, most of them are employed as either secretaries or clerks, mostly in commerce, or as teachers and nurses.

A breakdown of employees by industrial sector shows that about 30 per cent were employed by the commercial sector in Uganda and Tanganyika, and about 34 per cent in Kenya. Manufacturing was the next most important source of employment in Uganda and Tanganyika, while in Kenya transport and communications was an equally important source. The transport sector accounted for 15 per cent of Asian employees in Tanganyika, while agriculture, including cotton ginning and coffee curing, provided 12 per cent of the employment in Uganda. Public and other services were also fairly important sources of employment in all the three countries. We therefore find that one out of every three wage and salary earners is employed by the commercial sector, while the other employees are fairly evenly distributed among manufacturing, transport and communications, and services.

It is, however, more revealing to analyse the occupational distribution of employees in the three territories. Although this information is available only for Asian male employees in Uganda, I believe it is fairly representative of East Africa as a whole. The 1962 figures for Uganda show that out of about 9,000 male Asian employees, over 30 per cent did clerical or secretarial jobs, 16 per cent were employed in an administrative, executive or managerial capacity, while 11 per cent had professional and technological qualifications. Skilled 'manual' workers such as sales staff, carpenters, bricklayers, mechanics, etc. accounted for a further 30 per cent of total employees. These figures do not take account of the occupations of the self-employed and employers among the Asian community. There is little doubt, however, that the great majority of the persons in these two categories would be classified as administrative, executive or managerial personnel; a further substantial minority would consist of technologists and other professional persons. On the basis of observation and whatever little statistical evidence is available on the subject, we may hazard a guess that about 35 per cent of all the Asian workers perform executive, administrative or managerial functions, perhaps another 25 per cent are engaged in what we have described as 'skilled manual' jobs; a further 20 per cent do secretarial and clerical jobs, and about 15 per cent can be described as engaged in professional and technical occupations. It will, therefore, be seen that the majority of Asian workers furnish 'middle-level manpower' to the East African economies, while their contribution to the 'high-level manpower' is also substantial and growing rapidly. One remarkable feature of the Asian manpower in East Africa is the relative paucity of 'unskilled' persons among its ranks. The implications of the occupational distribution of the Asian labour force for future employment opportunities are far-reaching and will be discussed in detail in a subsequent section.

Before we come to a general assessment of the contribution of Asians to the economic development of East Africa, it is necessary to say something about their standard of living and distribution of income. Once again, we have more information on the average earnings of wage and salary workers than of the self-employed and the employers. In the case of Kenya, an analysis of the Graduated Personal Tax returns reveals the following pattern of income distribution by race:

Percentage of taxpayers in each income group by race: 1962

Income Group		Africans	Arabs and Somalis	Asians	Europeans
Under £120	..	91.4	86.0	11.0	1.5
£120—159	..	4.7	7.2	4.3	3.2
£160—199	..	1.7	1.9	3.3	0.6
£200—399	..	1.7	2.0	13.0	2.5
£400 and over	..	0.5	2.9	68.4	92.2
TOTAL	..	100	100	100	100

Source; Development Plan, 1964-70.   Kenya p.34.

The main weakness of the above table from our point of view is that the last income group ends at incomes of £400 and above; we do not, therefore, have any information on the income distribution of persons earning more than £400 a year. Nevertheless, the table reveals some interesting patterns; it shows that roughly one out of every three Asian workers earns less than £400 p.a. Perhaps even more revealing is the fact that no less than 11 per cent of the Asian tax-payers, or about 5,385 persons, had an income below £120 p.a. in 1962. It is forgotten too often that a substantial minority of the Asian population in East Africa has income levels barely sufficient to provide for the basic needs of the family. The table also brings out the great disparities in the income levels of different races.

There are reasons to believe that the average income of Asians in Uganda and Tanganyika is higher than in Kenya. As we shall see below, the average earnings of Asian employees both in Uganda and Tanganyika are higher than in Kenya; furthermore, as compared with the other two countries, a higher proportion of the Asian workers in Kenya are employees. Since the average income of employers and self-employed tends to be higher than that of the employees, we may conclude with reasonable certainty that the per capita income of Asians in Kenya is lower than that of their brethren in the rest of East Africa.

The above sketchy picture of the distribution of income among the Asians of East Africa needs to be supplemented by some qualitative observations. There is a very small layer of the Asian population in East Africa which can justifiably be described as 'affluent' even by the standards of the richest nations of the world. This group consists of a handful of industrialists, plantation-owners— sisal in Tanganyika, and sugar in Kenya and Uganda, coffee curers and cotton ginners in Uganda, owners of large department stores and import houses, and a few professionals such as highly successful barristers, doctors, architects and engineers. Their great affluence is underlined by their chauffeur-driven limousines, beautiful and spacious houses, lavish entertainment and frequent trips abroad to Europe, India and Pakistan. The great majority of Asians in East Africa, however, fall in what might be described as 'middle income group' with incomes ranging from £300 to £900 p.a. This group consists of most wage and salary earners, a sizable number of professionals and a great majority of retail traders dotted all over East Africa. The standard of living in this group varies considerably; at one extreme are those in the upper reaches of this income bracket, who lead a reasonably comfortable life and may enjoy the luxury of a motor car and other consumer durables. But perhaps a majority of persons in this group make do with a minimum of such comforts and may have to confine their recreation to listening to radios and transistors, or to an occasional visit to cinemas. For the most part, persons in this group would live in two to three roomed flats, in contrast to the spacious and well-laid-out houses of their more affluent brethren.

Lastly, there is a sizable and growing group of persons who may without exaggeration be described as indigent. This group usually consists of persons with large families, living in overcrowded slums, barely succeeding in making their two ends meet with an average family income of well below £200 p.a. Most of the members of this group constitute the core of the semi-skilled or unskilled section of the Asian labour force; some eke out a living from a small retail business located on the outskirts of urban areas or in the remote outlying districts. It is this section of the Asian working population which is often ignored in the popular as well as the more serious accounts of the Asians in East Africa.

The above account of the income distribution among Asians may be made more concrete by reference to the average earnings of Asian employees in the three East African countries. It was shown above that employees constitute a little more than half of the total Asian working population. An account of changes in their earnings would therefore provide an important evidence of changes in the economic well-being of the Asian community as a whole. Kenya has the best statistics on employment and earnings, which go back to 1948. These figures show that between 1948 and 1960, the index of average earnings rose from 100 to 189 for Asians, from 100 to 199 for Europeans, and from 100 to 268 for Africans. Thus the average earnings at current prices had slightly less than doubled for Asians between 1948 and 1960. In order to determine the increase in real earnings during this period, we adjust the 1960 figures by the Nairobi Cost of Living Index. This adjustment shows that the real average earnings for Asians have only increased by 20 per cent between 1948 and 1960.

The statistical evidence from Uganda also supports the hypothesis that the rise in average Asian earnings has been slower than that for either Europeans or Africans. Between 1958 and 1962, earnings per head for Asians increased by a mere 9.2 per cent, while the corresponding increases for Europeans and Africans were 22.9 per cent and 53.3 per cent respectively. The main reason for this disparity in wage and salary increases between the three communities is perhaps to be sought in the fact that whereas the wage level for Asians is determined essentially by economic factors, that for Europeans and Africans is influenced considerably by non-economic factors. The rise in Asian wages has been kept in check throughout East Africa by a general decline in employment in recent years as well as by increasing competition from the rising class of educated Africans. African wages, on the other hand, despite a contraction of demand, have shown a rapid upward trend mainly because of the successive minimum wage laws and the progressive Africanization of the better paid jobs. European salaries are determined more by the salary structure in U.K. than by the local economic conditions; hence an adequate explanation for changes in European earnings, which would be beyond the scope of this paper, has to be sought in relation to similar changes in the U.K.

However, these differences in the increase in earnings between the three races are quite insignificant in comparison with the great racial disparities in the level of average earnings. In Tanganyika, the average cash earnings for Asian males amounted to £564 p.a. in 1962; the corresponding figures for European and African males were £1,560 and £75 respectively. A study of earnings in Kenya and Uganda tell a similar story. Our main interest, however, is in Asian earnings. For purposes of comparison, it may be noted that the average cash earnings of Asian males in Kenya amounted to £551 in 1962 and in Uganda to £592. A study of the Asian wage structure in the three East African countries brings out two interesting points. First, the average earnings of Asian women are in general far below the men, especially in the private sector: in Uganda, average earnings of Asian males in the private sector at £561 p.a. compare with average earnings for females of £398. Secondly, the average earnings in the public sector are well above those of the private sector in all the three countries; to take our example from Tanganyika, the average earnings of Asian males in the public sector amounted to £776 p.a. in 1962, while the figure for the private sector was £497. The main reason for this disparity is undoubtedly the possession of higher skills by employees in the public sector, thus enabling them to command higher salaries.

We shall round off our discussion of the income distribution of Asians in East Africa by emphasizing the limitations of using average income figures as an index of economic welfare. Once again the Kenya data is the most comprehensive in this respect and will be used to illustrate our point. An average earning of £551 p.a. for Asian males obscures the fact that a very substantial proportion of the male employees had much lower incomes; in Kenya on less than 33 per cent had earnings below £360 p.a. Finally, it may be of interest to note that in the private sector (outside agriculture) only 8 per cent of the Asian males earned £900 or more per annum, compared with 84 per cent of European men; in the public sector the corresponding figures were 10 per cent for Asians and 92 per cent for Europeans.

We shall now attempt a general assessment of the contribution of Asians to the economic development of East Africa. The distinctive Asian contribution to the development of East Africa can best be understood and appreciated within the framework of a series of restrictions placed on the economic activities of Asians in the colonial period. These restrictions had the effect of confining Asian economic activities to certain limited industries and geographical areas; they go a long way in explaining the current pattern of geographical and occupational distribution of Asians in East Africa. We shall mention here only the most important of these restrictions. In Kenya and Uganda, Asians were precluded from owning and cultivating land, thus denying them any openings in the agricultural sector. This restriction was reinforced by a series of ordinances in the three countries preventing Asian traders from conducting business outside specified cities and townships. These two measures effectively prevented Asians from establishing a foothold in the rural economies of East Africa; however, they did not altogether stop certain economic transactions between Asian traders and African rural dwellers. Lastly, there was considerable discrimination against Asians in public employment throughout the colonial period. The formal aspect of this discrimination stopped in 1955 with the abandonment of a racial salary structure in the public services of the East African countries. But a series of administrative rules combined with accumulated prejudice to keep the Asians from the top executive and administrative posts in the civil service. It is, therefore, not surprising that the best energies and ability of the Asian population have tended to be concentrated on the fields which are open to them—trade, industry, the professions and skilled employment.

Historically, the most important contribution of Asians to the East African economies has been the extension of the monetary economy into the subsistence areas—a prerequisite for any economic development. A whole array of early explorers, administrators, and missionaries testify to the indispensability of Asian traders and artisans in the opening up and development of the interior. Their function was essentially the introduction of attractive imported consumer goods to large sections of the rural population throughout East Africa, thereby stimulating their desire for money incomes; until recent times Asian traders also acted as the main outlets for produce from the indigenous rural economies. Asian dominance in the distributive sector of the economy laid them open to charges of exploitation, which will be discussed later. Here it is important to emphasize that Asians continue to perform the old but vital function of introducing and extending the money economy in such areas.

Since the Asian *dukawalla* or shopkeeper is still a characteristic feature of townships and small urban centres throughout East Africa, it is necessary to say something about him. To a typical *dukawalla* living in a remote township, life offers few excitements, and hard work little compensation. The working day is long, usually starting at 7 a.m. and continuing late into the evening. The shopkeeper, who generally lives in a small brick house adjoining the shop, will typically be helped in his chores by his relatives; but he may barely manage to save enough for his children's education or for his daughter's dowry.[3] Life in the township offers few amenities; there is very little by way of organized recreation and entertainment.

The tedium of enforced leisure may partly and occasionally be relieved by social calls on the few Indian families in the neighbourhood. But in general there is little colour or variety in a dreary routine.

However, contrary to some popular myths held abroad, not all Asians in East Africa are *dukawallas* living in remote parts of the country. Today their main economic contribution is the supply of high- and middle-level manpower and of capital. This combination of capital and technical know-how in one section of the population is a great potential asset to the economy. Unfortunately, we do not have adequate data to assess quantitatively this crucial contribution to the total stock of capital and skilled manpower. According to Guy Hunter's estimates, in mid-1961 there were 67,500 skilled persons in East Africa, divided into two categories: the first consisted of just over 18,000 professional men of graduate or equivalent level, senior administrators, and senior managers in commerce and industry; and the second covered about 49,500 in the next layer of skilled manpower, including technicians and sub-professional grades (for example, the second echelon in agricultural extension work), executive grades in the civil service, middle management in industry and commerce, and teachers with secondary education but without a university degree. Hunter's estimates show that Asians provided a little less than 40 per cent of the people in category I and about 50 per cent of those in category II, in the whole of East Africa.[4]

We have no information on the occupational distribution by race of high-and middle-level manpower in East Africa. But a few sample surveys and general observation suggest that in category I the Asian contribution is especially large in medicine, law, engineering, pharmacy, accountancy and business management generally. In category II, Asians provide most of the skilled, manual personnel such as mechanics, electricians, tailors, carpenters, salesmen and supervisors. A large proportion of persons in category I consist of European expatriates, whose numbers may be expected to decline rather sharply in future. Thus the limited flow of African trained manpower will be needed not only to provide for the needs of the expanding economy but also to make good the expected loss of European expatriate manpower. It is, therefore, clear that a simultaneous withdrawal of Asian skilled manpower from the country could deal a crippling blow to the economy and act as a serious constraint on the development potential of East Africa.

Asians have made an equally important contribution in the form of savings and capital for the expansion of the economy. It is true that when the Asians originally immigrated to East Africa they brought relatively little capital with them; but it is also true that the savings made by them could have been used to increase their consumption rather than accumulate capital. A high proportion of this capital was originally generated in commerce, but it has since been invested in most sectors of the economy, especially in the manufacturing and construction industries. Again it is not possible to quantify the share of Asians in the national stock of capital, but a rough idea of their contribution to economic growth may be obtained by mentioning the main economic activities in which they have been pioneer entrepreneurs. In Uganda, cotton ginning and coffee curing were long a complete Asian monopoly, though in the last decade or so African co-operatives have greatly increased their share. At the moment all the sugar produced in Uganda is grown on the plantations of two Asians, who are also the leading industrialists in East Africa; the growing steel complex in Jinja owed its inception to one of them. Likewise, the timber and saw-mill industries were originally developed in Uganda on the initiative of Asian businessmen. In Tanzania, many of the largest sisal and other plantations are owned by Asians; while in Kenya, they have contributed greatly to industrial expansion in the post-war period. It is in fact difficult to think of any significant sector in the East African economies where Asian capital, entrepreneurial ability and skills have not made an appreciable contribution.

The economic success of the Asian community in East Africa has been due to their possession of certain qualities essential for economic development. The early Asian settlers were imbued with quasi-Protestant ethics; they were remarkable for their strong commercial sense, capacity to work long hours, low propensity to consume, and passion for accumulation of capital. With the increase in riches, the new generation have relaxed their single-minded pursuit of wealth. Nevertheless, a substantial number of younger Asian businessmen possess in abundance many of the qualities that enabled their forefathers to amass large fortunes. The qualities noted above, while vitally important for economic development, are essentially 'unheroic' and are not likely to endear their possessors to other communities. Asians have had more than their share of criticism from Europeans in the past and increasingly from Africans. It is to this aspect of the problem that we must now turn.

For long, Asians had a virtual monopoly of wholesale and retail trade and the marketing of minor cash crops, especially in Uganda and Tanganyika. Their dominance in the distributive sector of the economy exposed them to widespread criticism for alleged dishonest practices and to charges of exploitation. It is difficult to define the latter term precisely; in most cases it is undoubtedly used as a term of abuse without referring to any specific practices. To the extent that it is not used simply as a term of abuse, it may be expected to refer to a variety of sharp practices from which Asian businessmen, like the businessmen of other races, cannot claim entire freedom. These may include the problem of short weight, misleading information, overcharging, or any number of other ways by which customers feel themselves cheated. But in a majority of cases, criticism is levelled against the widespread practice of bargaining in Asian shops.

Any system of bargaining must inevitably lead to the charging of different prices to different customers, and thereby to complaints of exploitation and racial discrimination. It is perhaps also true that many Asian traders have shown themselves more interested in quick profits rather than in steady, long-term gains, and have not hesitated to exploit temporary scarcities to make windfall gains. All these malpractices have served only to promote ill-will and distrust between the customer and the trader. It will be noticed that none of these practices are peculiar to Asian traders in East Africa; indeed they are the stock in trade of businessmen all over the world, especially in underdeveloped countries. But in East Africa, because of the dominance of Asians in wholesale and retail trade, criticism of such practices is often couched in racial terms.

At another level, Asians are sometimes accused of holding back the progress and participation of Africans in the economy of the country. It is undoubtedly true that the presence of a large, economically sophisticated community has had the effect of retarding African participation in the commercial sectors of the economy. But to argue from this that the absence of the Asian community would have resulted in generally higher levels of income for Africans is to commit an error in elementary economics. In the preceding section, it was shown that the Asians have made a vital contribution to economic development; it is difficult to believe that East Africa would have developed to anything like its present level without the full and active economic participation of Asians.

The above criticism can be reinterpreted to imply that Asian business firms have not consciously aided Africanization. There is undoubtedly much truth in this charge. Asians have for the most part been solely concerned with their own economic salvation; in the past they have spared relatively little energy for the economic advancement of Africans. The skills and training which Africans have acquired from Asian business firms have been the by-product of their employment with the latter rather than the result of a conscious attempt to promote the economic position of Africans. Having said this, it is difficult to see how it could have been otherwise. Most of the Asian firms are small, essentially family concerns; in many cases the employment of Africans in 'responsible' positions would have meant a loss of jobs for some members of the family— something very few Asians are prepared to accept. However, the old attitudes and habits are gradually breaking down in the face of pressure from African leaders and—only occasionally—in the pursuit of enlightened self-interest. Some Asians have started business in partnership with Africans; many of the larger commercial and industrial firms have initiated policies of Africanization. Towards the end of 1964, the (Asian) Dar es Salaam Merchants Chamber announced a comprehensive scheme to accelerate the participation of Africans in the commercial and industrial sectors of the economy through loans, partnerships, and training in commercial techniques.[5] Despite these recent moves, one cannot help feeling that the Asian response to the need to increase the share of Africans in wholesale and retail trade has not been sufficiently swift or thoroughgoing.

In recent years, the Asian community has been widely criticised for exporting capital. The imminence of independence in East African countries, accompanied as it was by widespread fears of a breakdown of law and order in Kenya and Uganda, led to a crisis of confidence among the immigrant communities, resulting in a fall in domestic investment and a large outflow of capital abroad. With the attainment of independence and the return of confidence, there has been a slight reversal of the above trends, but there are still many individual Europeans and Asians who continue to transfer abroad part of their current income. The response of the immigrant communities to conditions of uncertainty and fear of exchange control has been similar to that of the affluent classes all over the world. The only solution to this problem—the imposition of control on transactions in foreign exchange—has been successively rejected, by independent African governments as well as by the colonial governments. It is difficult to see how, short of foreign exchange control, the capital outflow can be stopped altogether.

What of future prospects? There is little doubt that the coming of independence will increasingly mean large shifts of income and assets from non-Africans to Africans. This has already been foreshadowed in the policy declarations of the ruling parties in the three countries. The recently published Development Plans of Kenya and Tanganyika attempt to translate these policies into concrete projects. Before we consider them in detail, it is necessary to point out that the achievement of high rates of economic growth in East Africa could greatly ease the economic problems of the Asian community, while a stagnant economy could have serious effects on their economic prospects. Their actions and attitudes could be a vital determinant of the rate of growth. Asian businessmen and industrialists are responsible for a significant proportion of total investment; if they do not pursue expansionist policies, the efforts of the East African governments to accelerate the rate of economic growth will be largely frustrated, thereby seriously exacerbating the economic problems of the Asian community.

A very high proportion of the Asian labour force in East Africa, amounting to between 60 to 70 per cent, derive their livelihood from commerce or from employment in the public sector. Here the economic prospects for Asians appear rather gloomy. An accelerated programme of Africanization in the civil services has already gone some way in redressing the past racial imbalances; it is likely to be pursued vigorously for some years to come. But Africanization by definition leaves little scope for either the recruitment or the promotion of Asians. Different categories of Asian employees will be affected differently; the most numerous category, consisting of clerks, typists, and others holding junior executive posts, will be hit hardest by programmes of Africanization. Those in the teaching profession, particularly in the secondary schools, should have relatively little difficulty in finding jobs over the next few years. With regard to other graduates and persons with professional qualifications such as accountants, doctors, lawyers, architects, engineers, dentists, and so on, the prospects for employment in the public services will depend entirely on governmental attitudes.

There is little doubt that for many years to come there is likely to be an acute shortage of skilled and educated manpower in both the public and the private sectors. But this does not mean that the Asians with the necessary qualifications will automatically be assured of employment. The East African governments have up till now shown no great enthusiasm for employing Asians, even where Africans with the requisite qualifications are not forthcoming. This has undoubtedly resulted in an outflow of educated Asian manpower to countries like Canada, the U.K., India and Pakistan. An intensification of this trend could be a severe setback to efforts to solve the manpower crisis.

For many years to come there will be ample economic opportunities in private practice for professional persons; this is especially true of professions for which Africans have hitherto shown little inclination, such as engineering, accountancy, architecture or pharmacy. But persons with such qualifications will always command an international market, and the lack of openings in East Africa need not spell economic disaster for them. In any case, they will always constitute a tiny minority of the total Asian working population.

In the private sector, many of the leading expatriate firms are pursuing a policy of Africanization at all levels, and are therefore reluctant to take on new Asian employees. It is unlikely that the Asian predominance in wholesale and retail trade will last for long. One of the aims of the Development Plans drawn up in the three East African countries is to increase rapidly and substantially the share of Africans in commerce. This is perhaps stated most clearly in Tanganyika's five-year plan, which specifies that the co-operative movement should expand to secure 10 per cent of the total turnover of wholesale trade by 1970; the target for retail trade is 10 per cent by 1970, and in the long run some 30 per cent to 40 per cent of the total volume.[6] The Tanzania Government has worked out a comprehensive scheme to implement these targets; and it also plans to place the marketing of all crops in the hands of co-operative societies or of African farmers. This would deprive Asian *dukawallas* of a valuable source of income. Similarly, the Kenya Development Plan puts forward various proposals to enhance the share of Africans in commerce and industry; the most important of these is the decision to establish a chain of People's Shops managed by the National Trading Company, which will be formed under the aegis of Kenya Industrial Development Corporation. In Uganda, too, plans are afoot to help African traders through loans, subsidized rents, training programmes, and so on. All these measures, if successful, would imply an absolute reduction in the turnover of wholesale and retail trade handled by Asian businessmen. Thus the commercial sector is unlikely to absorb the increase in Asian labour force.

The pressure of African competition is already beginning to make itself felt among small retail stores, especially in villages and other small centres, and has resulted in a drift of Asian traders to the towns and cities.[7] The indications are that this pressure will be further intensified, and in a few years time the erstwhile ubiquitous *dukawalla* may cease to be a part of the landscape in small urban centres. It is only the large import, wholesale and retail businesses owned by Asians which will continue to have a future in East Africa.

This leaves us with the industrial and agricultural sectors as possible openings for the increasing Asian labour force. Undoubtedly, a rapid growth of the manufacturing and construction industries could ease their unemployment problem. But here again, the resultant demand for unskilled and semi-skilled jobs would be largely satisfied by the existing African labour supply; while only a few Asians may expect to be employed in managerial and executive posts. Is there any considerable scope in agriculture? Although Asians were prevented by legislation from acquiring and cultivating land in the past, the old reasons for this discrimination no longer apply. Agriculture might therefore be thought of as a possible solution to the 'Asian problem'; however, for a variety of reasons, this seems most unlikely, even if such policies were adopted. The question of land arouses the deepest emotions among Africans and any suggestion of alienating land for Asian settlement would run into bitter opposition. Quite apart from that, Kenya has no substantial unutilized land capable of cultivation. Even if the other two governments were to encourage Asian settlement, it is doubtful whether many capable and enterprising Asians would take kindly to agricultural life. Nor is it reasonable to assume that the governments would be prepared to inject large sums of capital and technical know-how to make these schemes viable. It does not, therefore, seem to me that agriculture is likely to employ any substantial number of Asians.

The above analysis does not hold out hopes of a bright economic future for Asians in East Africa, to that extent it confirms the current widespread pessimism among the Asian community. Economic difficulties will perhaps manifest themselves in growing unemployment, pressures on average earnings, increasing economic competition from Africans, and generally in a gradual erosion of the many privileges which Asians have enjoyed in the past. But all this will have the effect of closing the economic gap between Asians and Africans and thus may contribute to racial harmony in East Africa. Furthermore, for some years to come there may be a substantial net emigration of Asians from East Africa to India, Pakistan and the U.K. The emigrants will consist for the most part of retired civil servants and businessmen, of unemployed and of those with little prospects for employment, and finally of those with high educational qualifications in search of better economic opportunities, just as their fathers were a generation ago. Some of the Asian economic problems will therefore be exported in this way. For those who choose to stay on, their most enduring guarantee must lie in their complete acceptance as East Africans. To this process of acceptance, they can make a powerful contribution by a genuine commitment to the ideals and aspirations of an independent East Africa.

The governments and people of East Africa must in turn be vigilant against incipient racialism. It will be a bitter tragedy for East Africa and indeed for the whole continent if racialist tendencies which are unfortunately in evidence in certain quarters gather momentum, and racialists gain the upper hand. There are very few countries in the world where racial minorities do not suffer discrimination in one form or another. One, therefore, ought not to judge East African countries by very harsh standards. But if racialism prevails in East Africa, will our leaders be able to hold up their heads at international conferences and condemn, in good conscience, the injustices and humiliations heaped on Africans in South Africa and Negroes in the United States? Let us, therefore, continue to hope that East Africans will be spared the anguish of seeing the ideals of equality and brotherhood they fought for and cherish, lie shattered at their feet.

References

1. Except where otherwise stated, the quantitative data used in this chapter is derived from the following publications:
   Annual Statistical Abstracts for Kenya, Uganda and Tanganyika.
   1948 population census in Kenya, Uganda and Tanganyika.
   1952 and 1957 census for non-Africans in Tanganyika.
   1959 population census in Uganda.
   1962 population census in Kenya.
   Annual reported employment and earnings in Kenya: 1948-62.
   Annual employment and earnings in Tanganyika: 1961-62.
   Annual enumeration of employees in Uganda: 1958-62.
   Economic and Statistical Review; March 1964.
   Kenya Statistical Digest, June 1964.

2. The term 'economically active population' refers to all persons working as employers, own-account workers, unpaid family workers and employees, as well as those currently unemployed but in search of jobs. It excludes housewives, students, children, retired persons, etc.

3. of R. H. Desai, 'The Family and Business Enterprise Among the Asians in East Africa', paper presented to the Conference of the East African Institute of Social Research, Makerere University College, 1964.

4. Guy Hunter: *Education for a Developing Region: a Study in East Africa*, Allen and Unwin, 1963.

5. *The Nationalist* (*Dar es Salaam*), 17 August 1964.

6. Tanganyika's Five-Year Plan for Economic and Social Development, Vol. 1 Preliminary Edition, April 1964, p. 47.

7. 'The big increase in the number of African shops . . . has taken place in the last ten to fifteen years'. In 1961 there were 36,157 African retailers licensed. 'Very few of these African shops are in towns or trading centres; almost all are situated in the interior'. In 1961 there were 10,090 non-

African retail businesses, and 3,921 wholesalers, of whom the great majority were Asians, with a small number of Europeans: 'though the Asian traders are less numerous than the African, they handle, even at the retail level, much the greater part of the business'. *A Survey of Wholesale and Retail Trade in Tanganyika* (Economist Intelligence Unit, London, 1962), pp. 19 and 36-7.

5. An Educational Survey

P. M. Rattansi and M. Abdulla

Development of Asian Education

Although the educational systems which have come into being in the three East African countries share many features in common, they also inevitably reflect circumstances peculiar to each country. That is as true of the educational systems as a whole, as of the racial segments into which they have hitherto been divided. In Asian education, this is most apparent in the extent to which educational facilities are provided by the governments, on the one hand, and by aided and unaided schools, on the other.

Thus, in Tanganyika, Asian education developed on a community basis, with little aid from the government until comparatively recently. Even now most of the educational facilities are provided by aided schools in primary and secondary education. That is less true of Uganda, where the government assumed increasing responsibility, at least for secondary education, since 1932. In Kenya, a much larger proportion of the children are educated in government schools.

No more can be done here than to suggest some of the factors which must be considered in accounting for these differences; but even an enumeration of these factors gives some indication of the pressures which have shaped educational policy. One major factor is the difference in the public policies which guided the administrations in the pre-independence period. In Tanganyika, the principle that non-African education was to be organized and financed primarily by the two main races concerned was enunciated early by the United Kingdom as the mandatory power. By contrast, there was a much earlier assumption of responsibility for the education of the immigrant communities in Kenya, a 'Crown Colony' since 1920; the Education Department was founded in 1911 (in Uganda, only in 1925, while Tanganyika had its first Director of Education in 1920). Besides differences in public policies, account must be taken of the pressure from the Asians for expansion of education and greater financial commitment from the government. Such pressure appears to have been greater in Kenya, where education was for many decades a key issue in Asian political agitation. Since the Asian population of Kenya is almost equal to that of the two other territories combined, the strength of numbers has given a special edge and intensity to the demand. But there are other factors which demand equal consideration. In Uganda and Tanganyika, there has tended to be a greater predominance of the trading and self-employed in the Asian occupational structure; as will be suggested below, there has been less appreciation of education beyond literacy among these groups until recent decades. In Kenya, employment in the public sector has been more important for Asians than in the two neighbouring territories, and a correspondingly greater appreciation of the importance of education for such employment is to be expected. Finally, the style of Asian politics which developed in the three countries must not be ignored. In Kenya, the reaction against the political activities of the powerful settler minority led to the early organization of an Asian political movement, which was able to act as a sounding-board and a pressure-group for Asian needs, in education as in other fields.

At the beginning of the century, when there were probably about 40,000 Asians in East Africa, there was little government provision for Asian education. The first Asian school in Kenya was one established by the Uganda Railway Authority, and it was taken over by the government in 1912. In Tanganyika, a small school for Asians was started after the First World War, without government assistance. A number of private schools came into existence in Uganda by 1920. Greater educational activity, private as well as governmental, became more marked in the 1920s, and it may be remarked that large-scale Asian immigration into East Africa came in the later half of that decade.

In 1925, a small grant-in-aid was given to three Asian schools by the Uganda Government for the first time, although such expenditure amounted to only £2,500 by 1930. In Tanganyika, there were 24 Asian schools with 1,731 pupils by 1928, all entirely built and supported by the community. After 1929, the government assumed increasing responsibility, while reaffirming its policy that the administration and financing of non-African education was primarily the function of the two races. As a result of the continuation of this policy, a different pattern has emerged, as compared with the two other countries. In 1948, general control over Asian education was handed over to an Indian Education Authority (there is similar provision for the European community); and Asian education was

financed in part from a special tax levied on the Asians. The contrast
is visible, above all, in the predominance of the aided schools,
which account for nearly two thirds of the primary school students
today; in Uganda, the aided and unaided schools include three
fifths, and in Kenya about half the primary school students.

The aided schools point to an important characteristic of the
educational system: the continued existence of privately-organized
schools which supplement (and in Uganda and Tanganyika
preceded) the facilities offered by government schools. Many of
these schools are operated by Asian sub-communities. In Tanganyika
in 1959, for example, there were reported to be 51 Indian Public
Schools, 54 Aga Khan Schools, and 16 schools associated with
other communities. In 1952, in Uganda, there were 77 primary
aided schools, of which 41 were Indian Public Schools, 31 Aga Khan
Schools, and five 'government-controlled' (a category brought
in to solve dissensions following the partition of the Indian sub-
continent).

Organization of educational facilities on a communal basis can
be paralleled by organization of other social services on similar
lines among the Asians. The pattern of immigration, whereby early
arrivals attracted relations and neighbours to the land of their
adoption; the paucity of government provision for social services in
a newly-settled country; concentration in a small number of urban
centres which brought together large numbers of each sub-
community : these strengthened organization on communal lines
among the Asians.

Communal organization has been specially important in the
education of girls. In Kenya, education is compulsory only for
boys between the ages of 7 and 15 in Nairobi, Mombasa and Kisumu;
but it is estimated that probably 90 per cent of boys and girls
of school-going age attend school. But in 1960, only 30 per cent
of the girls receiving primary education were in government schools,
compared with 68 per cent of the boys. In Tanganyika, in 1958,
14 per cent of the girls were in government schools, compared with
27 per cent of the boys. The differences are smaller in Uganda:
19 per cent of the girls, and 25 per cent of the boys, in 1960. These
figures show that Asian girls have tended to be educated, at the
primary level, in aided (and therefore often sub-communal) schools
for the most part.

In the development of Asian education it seems likely that it
was primary education which was the main concern of the trading
section in the beginning. Literacy and reckoning seemed sufficient,

and the cost of maintaining a son at school when he could be contributing to the family income in trade made secondary education appear a luxury. It was the civil servant family, conscious of the range of bureaucratic jobs opened by further schooling, which was more concerned to agitate for improved and extensive secondary education. However, there was a growing diffusion of awareness about the importance of secondary education, especially after the Second World War. Such diffusion may show variations by territory: it may be significant that the educational reports for Uganda and Tanganyika have continued to voice complaints, even into the 1950s, about the wastage of Asian students in the secondary standards, through their being absorbed into commerce; the great dearth of candidates for teacher training from these countries has also been explained by reference to the superior attraction of commerce.

However, as the Asian and European settlements in East Africa have ceased to be enclaves in an alien land, and developed into increasingly modern and sophisticated societies, so *pari passu* has come a multiplication of roles and functions which could only be performed by those who have at least received secondary schooling. The changing nature and complexity of trade and industry have tended to make the business community as conscious as the 'service' section of the need for a higher level of educational facilities in general.

The increasingly articulated demand for more secondary education has reflected the more complex skills demanded by a developing society. It was accompanied by greater appreciation of professional and university education. The absence of local higher educational institutions and the scarcity of professional skills has meant higher rewards and social prestige for professional men. In addition, although economic power has remained in the commercial and industrial section, leadership has tended to gravitate to professional men, whether in sub-communal affairs, or in legislative bodies.

Since the end of the Second World War, the economic prosperity of the war years, together with more generous government provision for scholarships and bursaries, led to a growing stream of Asian students going overseas for higher education. In 1945, there were 19 Kenya students studying abroad with government bursaries, of whom 11 were Asian; by 1960, there were an estimated 2,500 Kenya students abroad, of whom nearly half were Asian. As will be shown in more detail below, since 1956 the creation of local institution of higher education has attracted growing numbers of Asian students.

In concluding this brief survey of the development of Asian education, some remarks may be addressed to the role of education in promoting social change. The 'unintended consequences' of a western-oriented educational system upon a traditional culture, threatened with disintegration in an alien environment, constitute an important aspect of social change in East Africa. Almost within a generation, the Asian population has been wrenched from a traditional society, and has turned its sights to a western-oriented one. Education has played a key role in the transition. Any inquiry, for example, into the extent of change from the joint family to the nuclear family, with its profound social consequences, must devote attention to the impact of education, and especially of the education of girls.

It would, however, be misleading to see education as the sole mover in the transition from a traditional to a western-oriented society. In East Africa we must consider also the urban setting of Asian settlement, exerting its influence as a forcing-house of change; the weakening of the authority of the parental culture, and the values it enshrines, because of the absence of any dense network of kinship bonds extending beyond the first generation; and, in Kenya, European settlers, small in numbers, but setting the tone of the whole society, and constituting the core of the economic and administrative structure. Given such a setting, education is one among a set of factors which can initiate a whole series of far-reaching changes in goals and values, and lead over time to important modifications in the social structure and cultural system.

The present system

In 1947, an official inquiry into Asian education in East Africa was conducted by Mr. A. A. Kazimi, an eminent Indian educationist. The main conclusions of the Kazimi Report provide a convenient point of departure for analysing the present state of Asian education. These were:

(1)   Due to the cessation of building during the war and a continuing increase in population, all schools were overcrowded: 'There is terrible overcrowding even in the Government schools necessitating the practice of allowing children of certain age limits to attend school only $2\frac{1}{2}$ hours a day . . . . The real need is for schools and more schools.'

(2)   The quality of the teaching staff was poor. In Kenya, only one third of the teachers in government service had a degree

or any professional qualifications. Conditions were worse in aided schools. Out of 213 teachers in aided schools only 54 were matriculates, while 123 were non-matriculates. Teaching was 'poor, unimaginative and unpractical.'

(3) The courses of study were too literary and the pupils had little opportunity to use their hands. The Cambridge School Certificate examination dominated everything. There was an urgent need for some provision for technical education.

(4) Opportunities for higher education were very restricted. There were no local institutions of higher education. At the same time, admission to universities in the United Kingdom was barred, since the Asian schools did not provide 'advanced level' courses.

The Kazimi Report dealt with a situation which had been greatly aggravated by war time difficulties. In the years that have followed, there have been improvements over the whole range of problems mentioned above; but that does not deprive them of their significance as the points of greatest strain within the Asian educational system.

Overcrowding has continued to be a serious problem. The primary and secondary school population increased very fast in the decade 1948-58, although there has been some decline in primary school numbers since 1960 in all the three territories. The number of Asian students attending primary schools in Uganda more than doubled (109.6 per cent) in the seven years 1948-55, followed by a much slower increase of 4.36 per cent per annum between 1955-61. In Kenya, there was an increase of 77.3 per cent between 1948-58; it had dropped to four-fifth per cent per annum between 1958-62. It Tanganyika there was an 85.2 per cent increase during 1948-58, followed by a decline from 1959. In secondary school, there was an increase of 237.2 per cent in Kenya (including a spectacular increase of 131.6 per cent between 1948 and 1949) between 1948-53, and of 96.2 per cent in Tanganyika over the same period. In Uganda, there was an increase of 240 per cent between 1948-55, followed by a slower one, 100.8 per cent, between 1955-61. Comparable figures for the other two territories were: Kenya 198.4 per cent between 1953-62; Tanganyika, 147.1 per cent between 1953-61.

Coping with an expansion of such a magnitude demanded a massive programme of building, recruitment and training; but the response of the governments concerned proved slow and inadequate. In Kenya, the Development Committee in 1946 had suggested a five-year scheme to expand schools and teacher training centres.

The rapid increase in the school population, the rise in price levels, and increases in teachers' salaries rendered the original estimates out of date very soon. Buildings remained greatly overcrowded, classes were very large. A great many unqualified teachers had to be recruited, and a double-shift system was operated. It proved possible to abolish the double-shift system in Uganda by 1954; in Kenya it continued into the late fifties. The colonial government drew criticism from Asian representatives for allocating an unfair share of the revenue (proportionate to their tax burden) to the European community, while making grossly inadequate provision for the Asians. Suspicions were expressed that the results of the Kenya Preliminary Examination were deliberately 'doctored' so as to restrict the number of passes and, thus, access to secondary education to the Asian students.

In teacher training, Kenya gave a lead which was later followed by the other territories. In the past, the majority of teachers were recruited from India and Pakistan. It was gradually realized that East Africa must aim at self-sufficiency, at least as far as primary school teachers were concerned. It was necessary to establish institutions to provide teachers' training, and to supplement them by grants to students to enable them to qualify in the United Kingdom as secondary school teachers. In January 1949, an Asian men teachers' centre was opened at Nairobi, which was followed by a women teachers' training centre three years later. Neither could claim much initial success, and the main reason was undoubtedly the unattractiveness of teachers' salaries. Men teachers had to balance their choice against greater rewards and opportunities in commerce and industry. A significant number of Asian women had entered employment since the war; but in teaching they were entitled only to four fifths of the salary of male teachers in the corresponding scale. There were only 12 second-year students in the men teachers' centre by 1951, and no more than 16 girls had completed a two-year course at their centre.

Numbers improved steadily with the raising of teachers' salaries on the recommendation of the Lidbury Commission of 1954. Only one third of the teachers in government and aided Asian schools in 1954 had received any professional training; by 1957 nearly half the teachers were trained. In 1962, the three training colleges in Kenya had 261 students (65 men and 196 women).

Up to the end of 1958, there were no teachers' training facilities for Asians in Tanganyika. Students who had obtained a School Certificate were sent to the colleges in Kenya, the full costs of the training being met from the Tanganyika Education Fund: for example, there were 11 students in 1958, who completed their training the following year. In March 1959, a college was opened in Dar es Salaam and 20 young men and women admitted for a two-year course for primary school teachers.

Uganda, like Tanganyika, has experienced difficulties in attracting sufficient local Asians into teaching. In 1954, 16 completed the first year of a two-year teachers' training course at the Kampala Teachers' Training College; 26 were trained by 1956. The Education Department complained in 1957 that the output of Asian teachers' training was 'very far' from providing the numbers required. The 1959 Report, noting that there had been a 130 per cent increase in the Asian primary school population since 1952, declared bluntly: 'Any further expansion will depend on a more buoyant national income and the willingness of many more young Asians to train for the teaching profession.'

The efforts of the three territories to increase the proportion of qualified teachers can be traced through the years by an analysis of the relevant statistics:

Kenya			1950	1955	1960
With university degrees	..	..	20.7	31	33
Completed secondary schooling	..		49.6	47	46.8
Without secondary schooling	..		29.7	22	20.2

Excluding those with university degrees, untrained teachers were 73.5 per cent of all teachers in 1950, and 62.9 per cent in 1955; but the figure had dropped to 46.5 per cent in 1960.

Tanganyika			1951	1956	1961
With university degrees	..	..	25.1	35.1	42.9
Completed secondary schooling	..		35.7	44.7	46.8
Without secondary schooling	..		39.2	20.2	10.3

Excluding the first category, untrained teachers were 70 per cent of all teachers in 1951, 65.4 per cent in 1956, and 46 per cent in 1961.

Uganda				1955	1960
With university degrees	..	..	..	49.8	38.0
Completed secondary schooling	..	..	..	25.2	53.1
Without secondary schooling	..	..	..	25	8.9

Again, excluding the first category, untrained teachers were 56.6 per cent of all teachers in 1955; they had only dropped to 52.51 in 1960.

The Kazimi Report drew attention to the neglect of technical training, and greater provision has been made, especially in Kenya, over the years. In 1949, a purely communal institution, the Mombasa Institution of Muslim Education, was established to provide technical and trade education, and it had 103 students by the end of 1953. By 1954 there were two Asian technical high schools, in Nairobi and Mombasa, with 725 students. A landmark in the provision of technical education was the opening of the Kenya Polytechnic in 1961, for students in employment who usually attend one day plus one evening per week. It includes courses in science, engineering, building, commerce and domestic science. Asians formed 33.7 per cent of its students in June 1962. In addition, the two technical high schools had an enrolment of 1935 by June 1960. There has been a Technical Institute in Dar es Salaam since 1958, and an expanding institute in Kampala.

Opportunities for higher education were greatly restricted in 1947, and the lack of post-secondary education at the schools limited the number of students able to fulfil the minimum entrance requirements of English universities. These opportunities have expanded since then due to (*a*) provision for post-secondary education; (*b*) government loans and bursaries for higher education; and (*c*) the growth of a University of East Africa, with constituent colleges in the three territories.

The first post-secondary classes in Kenya began at the Prince of Wales School in Nairobi. Kazimi had suggested that the school, which was exclusively European, should permit some Asian students to take advantage of these facilities; but the suggestion was anathema to the European community of those days. The only other solution was that of starting post-secondary classes at the Asian schools; not until 1951 were such classes started at the Government Asian School in Nairobi. Owing to the lack of hostels, students from outside Nairobi were unable to make full use of the opportunity until the end of the 1950s.

The programme of bursaries and loans against securities was expanded. In 1949, the Kenya Government awarded bursaries and scholarships to the value of £2,820; the amount had risen to £8,610 in 1960. The figures below illustrate the growth of loans and bursaries, and their distribution among the three races:

Number of Government Bursaries held   Expenditure

	1960	1960/61	1961/2	1960	1960/61	1961/62
Europeans	53	56	53	£8,941	9,330	10,413
Asians	62	75	80	£8,610	9,925	11,225
Africans	28	34	40	£16,505	26,390	30,085

Number of Loans for Higher Education Overseas

			1960	1961	1962
Europeans	..	..	29	33	35
Asians	..	..	63	77	72
Africans	..	..	32	35	46

There was a small provision in Tanganyika for bursaries. The triennial survey for 1955-57 reported that there were 185 Asian students in the United Kingdom, but only nine of them were in receipt of government bursaries. From Uganda, in the same year, there were 41 Asian bursars in the United Kingdom and 12 in India.

Local facilities for higher education have developed gradually. Makerere, the first institution of university status in East Africa did not attract many Asian students, probably because in its earlier stages it was meant exclusively for Africans. A report in 1952 pointed out that 'a small quota at Makerere College is available for non-Africans, but so far, very few of them have been taken up. The Asian population, therefore, relies almost entirely for higher education on universities in India and Pakistan and the United Kingdom.'

The need for a university college for all races was fully realized by the Asians, and the Kenya Asian community decided to build such a college in memory of the great Indian leader, Mahatma Gandhi. The arduous task of raising the large funds required for the purpose was undertaken by an Indian scholar, Dr. Yagnik. Meanwhile, in 1953, the Kenya Government formed an Advisory Council for Higher Education, and it was decided that the proposed Royal Technical College in Nairobi would function on a non-racial basis. The Gandhi Memorial Academy Committee thereupon decided to merge its plans into those for the new college and transferred the substantial funds it had collected to the college. As a result, the Gandhi Memorial Academy came to be incorporated with the Royal Technical College, which admitted its first students in 1956. Of the 157 Kenya students in that year, 94 were Asian, 57 African, and 6

European. By 1960, the number of Asian students from Kenya was 106. The college is now known as the University College, Nairobi, and, together with Makerere College, Kampala, and the University College, Dar es Salaam, forms part of the new University of East Africa.

The establishment of the University of East Africa has given a greater number of Asian students, in common with students of other races, access to higher education. But it is to be expected that the majority of those seeking higher education will continue to make the United Kingdom and India and Pakistan their destinations. The relative unimportance of local institutions, as compared with those abroad, is shown by some recent figures for Asian students from Kenya and Tanganyika:

Asian higher education

Kenya	U.K.	India and Pakistan	Makerere	Nairobi	Others
1960/61	847	520	31	92	30
1961/2	905	800	37	87	44
Tanganyika					
1960/61	394	4	16	22	14
1961/2	477	6	20	28	18

The Future

With the coming of independence to East Africa, many new problems have arisen in the field of Asian education; and most of the old problems remain[1]. For the Asian community the need to acquire education has increased just as the opportunities to acquire education are diminishing. Asian survival to some extent is contingent on the attainment of high technical skills. Employment at the semi-skilled or clerical level will be difficult; nor is it likely that in the future many youngsters will be absorbed in family business and shops. On the other hand, the needs of the countries for skilled manpower is unlikely to be met from Africans locally, and qualified Asians not only should have no difficulty in finding employment, but could also very significantly and positively help in the development of these countries. There is and there may for some time continue to be, a prejudice in government and big foreign commercial firms against Asians, even though they possess the requisite qualifications. But the world scarcity of skilled manpower and the inability of the economies to support a large expatriate staff may mitigate this prejudice. Moreover, even if these qualified Asians do not find acceptance in East Africa, it would be quite easy for them to move to other parts of the world where their services are in demand. It is therefore vital for the Asians that they acquire high educational qualifications, especially of a technological kind.

The control of education is primarily in the hands of the governments, and in this sense the future of the Asians is also in the hands of the governments. If the governments adopt policies which discriminate against the Asian school children and effectively reduce their opportunities for education, the future for the Asians will be terribly bleak. In the past the Asians had more favourable educational opportunities than Africans. The educational systems were organized on a racial basis, with well-nigh total segregation.

One of the most exciting challenges of independence is the integration of the educational system. Educational policies in future should no longer be tied merely to communal needs and circumstances, but should be based on the best interest of the country as a whole. Henceforth there should be no such thing as 'European Education', 'Asian Education', 'African Education', 'Arab Education'. In this process of integration, Asian advantages *vis-à-vis* the Africans must disappear. In Kenya, for example, education for Asian boys was compulsory in the urban areas between the age of 7 and 15; but this was repealed in 1963, as an instance of discriminatory practice since no such rule applied to the Africans. Also, till recently most Asian children who had obtained primary schooling could go on to the secondary school, whereas in the African educational system there was a serious bottleneck between primary and secondary schools. Integration of secondary schools will mean a re-allocation of secondary school places, and the Asian share must diminish. Asian share will diminish even if entry to the secondary schools is made competitive on an academic basis; but it is clear that the governments will introduce other kinds of control as well on Asian children.

In Tanganyika, for example, quotas are prescribed for secondary schools and an Asian child (who may be a citizen) has greater difficulties than an African child. Conditions for non-citizens are even more stringent. The result of this would be growing illiteracy among the Asians[2], with all its consequences, or a massive effort on the part of the community to provide supplemental educational facilities. There is already among the sections of the Asian community a tradition of communal education institutions. There is no reason why this tradition should not be broadened and a collective Asian effort not be made to provide schools and scholarships. Obviously these facilities cannot be made exclusive to Asians, but a great proportion of them ought to benefit. The Asian community of East Africa has always set great store by education, and has sacrificed much so that their children might go to schools and colleges. Now in these difficult times, they ought again to concentrate their resources on providing facilities for education.

Another range of problems is connected with higher education. In the period which immediately preceded independence, and in that following independence, 'crash-programmes' of scholarships from overseas countries have resulted in a large number of African students going abroad for higher education. The large intake in African primary schools in recent years will result in a 'bulge' in the secondary schools, and a great pressure on higher education, in future. The competition for limited places in university colleges and polytechnics in East Africa may therefore be expected to affect Asians increasingly in future. Thus, there are likely to be difficulties in securing admission to local institutions just when the ability of parents to finance overseas education may be decreasing.

Asian students going abroad for higher education in the period just after the Second World War tended at first to concentrate on a narrow range of subjects, specially law and medicine; later more students chose such subjects as architecture, pharmacy, optics and accountancy. At present, there is a sharp contraction in the number of those choosing law and architecture, while probably medicine, science degrees, and, especially, engineering show an expansion. The changes show the responsiveness of educational choice to the changing occupational opportunities in East Africa. In future, the choices of Asian students will obviously have to conform much more closely to the needs of developing East Africa.

Another result of the shortage of school places will be the growth of private schools. By private schools is meant those schools which have no government aid. If a school obtains any aid from the government, then it becomes liable to be ordered by the governments, and in Tanzania communal schools which receive some assistance from the government have to accept government instructions about the intake of students according to race. But private schools have so far been free from this kind of control. The private schools have a very definite function to perform, but there are some dangers that need to be guarded against. There is the danger, for example, that these schools might become purely commercial enterprises in which educational aims are subordinated to the urge to maximize profits. Staffing will be a problem, and poor quality teaching is all too likely. There will be the temptation to admit a larger number of students than the school can cope with. Overcrowding and inadequate facilities will be the result. Thus while the need for private schools exists, a great effort is needed to ensure proper standards, honesty and absence of exploitation; it may become necessary to take these schools out of commercial hands; and increasing government control might also become inevitable.

Other important consequences of integration of schools should be noted. The scarcity of secondary school places will result in some Asian families emigrating from East Africa if their children cannot get education here; the beginnings of this trend are already obvious. However, by far the most important consequence of integration will be on race relations. It is at this stage difficult to say what the effects will be, since integration has only just begun, but certain predictions might be made from experience elsewhere. Integrated education ought to lead to greater racial understanding; interracial friendships might grow before there is time for race consciousness and prejudice to emerge. Social contacts between the parents may not increase very much, but some African children will have access to Asian homes and *vice versa*. This could be the turning of the tide.

The integration of schools will be accompanied by some revision of the syllabus. Swahili is now compulsory in Kenya and Tanzania for all children. This fact is extremely important for purposes of social integration; language has been to some extent a barrier in the past; Swahili is becoming the national language and a pride in its use, obvious. Were the Asians to continue to display an ignorance of Swahili, they would give additional cause for suspicion and non-acceptance, and effectively reduce for themselves opportunities in government and private service. With the rise of Swahili, there is bound to be the decline of the Indian languages. This in turn will have an impact on social and cultural structure of the Asians and make social integration more possible. Even though all the governments are pledged to the principle of religious instruction, a certain amount of secularization is inevitable; this again is relevant for Asian attitudes and behaviour.

Education is crucial not only for the Asians but for everyone else in the countries as well, for the goals of nation-building and quick economic and social development which these countries have set for themselves. Already various studies have been made to estimate the manpower requirements, especially among the high-

and middle-grade personnel, entailed by the growth-rate targets.

The educational implications of these plans may be illustrated by the development plan for Kenya, which covers the period from 1964 to 1970. Basing itself on the Hunter Report of 1963, it estimates that 103,000 highly-trained people would be needed by 1971, assuming a 'normal' rate of growth. The figure would represent an increase of 45,000 over those similarly employed in 1961, as well as another 22,000 to replace those retiring or emigrating. Of the needed personnel, it is proposed to train 60,000 in Kenya. The magnitude of the expansion involved is shown by the fact that it would mean two and a half times as many Form IV school-leavers in 1970 as there were in 1963. The plan states that the government 'accepts as a second major objective in the resources field the rapid expansion of secondary level education, the assurance of university places to qualified students and the provision of managerial and technical training and increased opportunities in commerce, industry and agriculture'.

On this level, the Asian role in the educational systems of East Africa is likely to increase. There is an acute shortage of teachers, especially at the secondary school levels. The attractions for qualified Africans in the non-teaching professions are too handsome, and these pose a real problem in recruiting graduate African teachers. More and more Asian graduates, on the other hand, are going into the teaching profession. With the integration of not only the students but also the staff, increasing numbers of Asian teachers will be teaching African students—hitherto an unknown phenomenon. Africans have great respect for teachers, and it is possible that the Asian effort in the education process will help improve their image. Teaching may become the key role of the Asians. Also, the new Asian teachers will be local Asians, unlike the former generation of Asian teachers who were recruited from India and Pakistan. These new teachers are fully aware of the race tensions and Asian dilemmas; most of them are sympathetic to the cause of African progress. Theirs is a challenging task, and their opportunities are considerable.

References

1. The problems which continue to overshadow Asian education in East Africa are those which the Kazimi Report noted two decades ago: overcrowding, with its attendant evils of large classes and lack of individual attention; financial limitations on building, and on training and staffing; selection procedures for secondary education, especially the K.P.E. in Kenya.

2. In the new context, the problem of Asian students who fail to enter secondary schools is part of the larger problem of *all* students who fail to do so, since the aim must be that of making best use of the human potential they provide. The difficulties which can arise in developing a common policy are shown by an example from Uganda. There it was decided some years ago that post-primary schools should be established for such students to train them in agriculture, through rural farm and trade schools. As land is not available for Asians, such schools could not meet their needs. The Uganda Education Report for 1957 commented that, apart from those whose parents were able to provide professional training overseas, the rest of the Asian students went into trade, or such occupations as untrained motor mechanics, neglecting assistant-level job training in various government departments, and the training provided by the technical schools now open to all races.

6. The Future Prospects

Yash P. Ghai

The preceding chapters have given a picture of the Asians in East
Africa in relation to their social, economic, political and educational
status. In attempting to discuss the prospects of the Asians in the
future in East Africa, this picture will need to be kept in mind. It
points to both the strength and weakness of the community in
meeting the problems that face it. The problems that the Asians
face are numerous and difficult. The Asians are an immigrant
minority, small in numbers, marked out by race and wealth, in a
newly independent African country whose leaders are determined on
a policy of wide-scale change. The policies of these leaders are
concerned not merely with increased wealth and rapid economic
development, but much more importantly, with effecting fundamental structural changes in their societies, which would involve
the reallocation of what have become traditional roles of the different
communities in East Africa, and of generating increasing social and
economic mobility for the Africans. Understandably, the primary
interest of the new governments is the welfare of Africans; it would
appear that in the formulation and execution of these policies,
these governments are not going to be significantly concerned with
the consequences for the Asians. Nor can the Asians, unlike the
European minority, expect help from outside countries; India and
Pakistan will not come in unless the situation so deteriorates that an
evacuation operation is necessary (as in Zanzibar after the 1964
revolution). It will be for the Asians to work out for themselves
their place in an increasingly fluid and changing society.

There is no evidence to suggest that the governments will necessarily be unsympathetic to the attempts by the Asians to find a place in a
changed order; but it is unlikely that the governments will undertake
to suggest solutions of the Asian problems. This makes it imperative
for the Asians to think of their place and roles in the colonial East
Africa and in an independent East Africa. It is quite irrelevant
whether or not they want to change their place and role, except to
indicate the magnitude of the problems of transition, for the choice

is not theirs. If they want to stay in East Africa, a revision is a prerequisite; those who have been unwilling to make this revision have already left the country or else are contemplating doing so.

Quite what adjustments the Asians will have to make depends on a correct identification of the problems and areas of conflict with the Africans. This in turn, at least partially, depends on the policies of the new African governments. That it should have been necessary to identify the areas of conflict by reference to the policies of the African leaders in itself highlights some aspects of the problem; a failure on the part of the Asians to do independent thinking in this matter, and, partly as a result of this failure, a lack of initiative from the Asians, with the result that instead of presenting the country with positive policies and action to reduce racial tension, they just have had to step aside and accommodate themselves to government-sponsored measures to promote an increased role of Africans in the different spheres in the country's life. And even now the Asian role is somewhat passive; its contribution seems at best to be one of accommodation (and even this view is challenged by some African politicians who have often accused Asians of obstruction). There does not appear to be a positive contribution by the Asians, an enthusiastic commitment and assistance to the policies and plans of the government. To some extent this attitude is understandable, for most of these policies are aimed at undermining their economic status, and not to obstruct is an act of sacrifice; and also because the governments have not encouraged positive contribution by Asians. Nothing like adequate use has been made of Asian skills and expertise; the governments have preferred to engage expatriates at enormous salaries to employing local Asians with skills comparable to those of the expatriates.[1] The absence of significant Asian involvement in the tasks of development is as much due to the attitude of the African leaders as it is to the attitude of the Asians.

What then are the policies of the new governments? Their basic purpose is an improvement in the lot of the Africans, and increased control of public and private institutions by the Africans. These policies range over a wide area of activities: education, public services, commerce and trade, agriculture. Preference in all these areas is given to Africans, and active governmental assistance in areas which are often in other countries left to private enterprise.[2] In one country or another of East Africa, these areas are crucial to the Asians; and the government policies directly affect the continuance of the Asian role in these areas. On a more general level, the government policies are aimed at creating strong, centralized governments, with powerful trends towards one-party states, which demand absolute loyalties, insist on uniformities, and are suspicious of any kind of dissent. The Asian political role in this context will have to be a cautious one; it might naturally be quite passive, but the governments will not be content with mere passivity; they would expect active support. On race relations, the avowed government policies are to eliminate discrimination and in attempting to generate sentiments of nationhood, to underplay differences of race and tribe. They want racial integration, but beyond pointing out that the immigrants will have to revise some of their attitudes, they have not defined integration. The word 'assimilation' has been little used. Precisely what is expected in this delicate area is not clear; and it is obvious that the Asians face difficult problems here.

Before the details of these policies and their implications are discussed, it is useful to mention the Asian attitudes and the obstacles that face the Asians in any process of adjustment. It must be stated at once that it requires a real effort on the part of the Asians to change to new conditions. It is so not merely because, in the short run at any rate, many changes are bound to affect the majority of them adversely, but also because the Asian is set in his ways of thought, living and social organization. In this he was encouraged by the former régime. One of the most striking features of the colonial rule was the compartmentalization of society in three or so racial groups, a compartmentalization which was reinforced by economic, social and political discrimination and segregation. There were separate residential areas for the different communities, separate schools, hospitals, maternity homes, clubs; on the political level, the institution of separate electoral communal representation stimulated racial political parties and made racial interests inevitable as political issues; and the nominated majorities in the legislative councils, and so the absence of a genuine parliamentary cabinet system made less imperative forms of racial co-operation among the elected communal members and their political parties. On the economic level, the compartmentalization was reinforced by differential scales of salaries in the public, and imitatively, the private sectors, the exclusion of non-whites from the White Highlands; the African reserves; the lack of equal opportunities in public and private services; the necessity for Africans to have '*kipande*'[3], etc. if they wished to stay in towns. The result was to preserve and strengthen the political, economic and social dominance of Europeans, with Asians occupying the middle, and the Africans the bottom place in this system. The effect of all this was to make the

Asians inward-looking, and to organize schemes of self-help to supplement deficiencies in government provision of schools, hospitals, etc. Those schemes of self-help were very largely, though not exclusively, for the Asians.

It is clear that such a system was not erected for the benefit of the Asians. Yet, though there was some opposition to it, there was a wide measure of acceptance. Why was this? There were various reasons. On the social level, the colonial compartmentalized system suited the Asian temperament. The Asians are extremely communal-minded, conscious of caste differences, intensely endogamous. Both the pluralism of cultures in India and the divisions within the Asian community in East Africa illustrate this point. The Asians wanted to be left alone to pursue their own traditional ways and thus to maintain their culture. Laws were enacted in East Africa providing for the application of personal, religious laws, e.g., marriage, divorce, succession, to the Asian religious communities. This helped not only to preserve the cultural identity of these communities, but also put obstacles in the way of inter-communal and inter-racial contacts. In addition, the Asians, by and large, continued to maintain links with their countries of origin; as far as the government and some big commercial firms are concerned, this was helped by fairly generous provisions for 'home' leave every four years or so. Also, for a long time there was immigration from India, and the immigrants tended to come from certain specified regions of India, the Panjab and Gujarat, which had already provided the bulk of the Asian community. The effect of all this was to make the Asians a self-sufficient, ethnocentric community. This factor today consitutes one of the main obstacles to a meaningful integration of communities.

Another reason the colonial system was accepted was that by defining areas of occupation and activity on a racial basis, it made it easier for the Asian to identify his role, and as he was an immigrant, unsure of his rights and status, he was probably grateful to be spared the pains of transition and the tensions of racial conflict and competition. And, though he knew that certain positions of eminence were closed to him, he was to a certain extent sheltered from competition from the African. It is surprising that there was not more resentment of the superior status and racial arrogance of the Europeans. In a curious way, the Asians had come to believe in the myth of white superiority. The pyramidical racial structure was sometimes taken too much for granted; it was proper and inevitable that in the order of things, the white men should be at the apex. Rather as a corollary of this attitude, and, partly as a rationalization of the better economic, social and political status of the Asians compared with that of the Africans, the Asians began to believe that the Africans were inferior to themselves. If the African got less wages than the Asian, if he had to live with the whole family in one small room—'the boys' quarters', if he had to walk miles or lift heavy weights, the Asian conscience was untroubled because the African was different, he was inferior; he was used to these things; he did not want and certainly would not know what to do with modern conveniences and gadgets. It is because now the same African, who they think has low intelligence and no experience, is in control of government that the Asian has tremendous problems of reconciling himself to the new order. It is one thing to accept the rule of a superior race, indeed, one even tries to imitate them, but how humiliating to be bossed around by members of an inferior race! Even though more subconsciously than consciously, the East African Asian has assumed attitudes of racial superiority *vis-à-vis* the African. Therefore today even if the Asian accepts the political supremacy of the African, he insists on his own superior culture and higher intelligence. Minorities can ill afford affectations of superiority *vis-à-vis* majorities which themselves are not totally free from inferiority complexes, even though a belief in the value of their culture is necessary for minority survival. The racial attitudes of Asians are clearly a big hurdle to overcome.

The Asians accepted the colonial set-up also partly because of a low political consciousness and little education. Sensitivity on matters of human rights are a relatively new phenomenon; and the older generation of Asian immigrants should not be too severely reprimanded for not caring enough for others. The younger generation are more conscious of issues of human rights and fairness and social justice. African nationalism is partly responsible for the stimulation of this new consciousness; African political agitation was based on principles of equality, justice and fair play. This factor also accounts for the disillusionment of some of the younger Asians. They actively supported or favoured African nationalism because it was based on these principles, even though this meant isolation in their own community, but some of them now have a feeling of betrayal; they feel that the African leaders have not lived up to these principles once they have attained power. Whether this feeling is justified or not is not an easy question to answer, but it is of some importance. The hopes of better racial understandings rest a great deal on these young Asians; their alienation from the ethos of the countries could be disastrous, for the Asians in particular.

The difficulties of the Asians are further intensified by the fact that they failed effectively to fight on behalf of, and later with, the Africans. Too much is perhaps made of the argument that the Asians allied with the imperialists. In a system where positions of eminence were secured through the dispensation of patronage rather than through popular support, it is inevitable that the so-called leaders of the Asian community (and also of the African) should appear to be in the pay of the imperialists. On the other hand, however, the Asian community's position has often been ambivalent. They have an impressive record of humane politics in the twenties and thirties. But with the imminence of African rule, Asian preoccupation with their own future became marked, and the possibility of the clash of their interests with those of the Africans led some to believe independence was not in their interest. Nevertheless, it ought to be pointed out that at worst the Asians were un-enthusiastic; they offered no active resistance to African progress to independence; and several of them actively supported the African politicians. (To some extent Asian political support was inhibited by the fact that the African political parties, by their own constitutions, confined membership to Africans). Although not widely appreciated, the early political activity of the Asians helped to prevent Kenya from becoming a South Africa or a Southern Rhodesia. They strenuously resisted European settler claims of Kenya being a white man's country. This effect of Asian activity is of cardinal importance for the whole of East Africa[4]. The Africans do not generally acknowledge this support given by the Asians; just as in the economic and social matters, the Africans deny that the Asians have made any significant contribution for the good, they under-rate Asian political contribution. Their assessment of the Asian political role tends to be coloured by their social and economic relations with the community.

The Asians are a more hated minority than the Europeans. There would seem to be various reasons for this. The Asians occupy positions which are the immediate aspirations of the masses of Africans; the European's position is as yet too elevated and too remote. Asian control of retail trade is particularly resented; there is a feeling among the Africans that the Asian traders have conspired together to hinder the participation of the Africans in commerce; and that were it not for this conspiracy, the Africans would rapidly and effectively engage in trade. This view overlooks the skills, experience and hard work that are needed to succeed in the retail trade. African accusations of exploitation by Asian traders are largely unrealistic; Asian *dukawallas* in remote parts of the country live on pitiful margins of profit; work enormously long hours, get the whole family to serve in the shop, live a life of austerity, cut off from many amenities of modern life, and retire after a long life's work with meagre savings. The image of the exploiting, unscrupulous, wealthy Asian class has been so popularized that the very real sacrifice and contribution of these small, up-country shopkeepers has been completely ignored, to be replaced by a long catalogue of sinful practices.

In a way it is ironical that the Africans should be more hostile to the Asians than to their former rulers. There is an important reason for this. One major point of conflict between the Europeans and Africans was the question of the occupation of land. This conflict has been considerably eased by the resettlement schemes which enabled many European farmers to sell their farms at generous prices, which were later transferred to Africans. Also the majority of the European civil servants were covered by compensation schemes which enable them to retire with grace and substantial sums. On the other hand there has been no similar scheme for the Asian civil servants. As far as retail and wholesale trade is concerned, there has not been any machinery to enable Asian traders to sell their businesses to make room for Africans. The schemes which enabled the Europeans to pull out of these countries were extremely expensive for East Africa.

Another reason the Asian minority has been specially marked out for hostility lies in its social structure, mention of which has already been made. Majority of the Asian-African relations have been at the shopkeeper—customer or master—servant level, neither of them calculated to inspire sympathetic understandings or good fellowship. The Asian social organization is closed to outsiders; whereas in towns, schools and universities, the African learns much of the European ways of life, the Asian ways remain a mystery. Also, while among the Europeans there have been missionaries, school-teachers, etc., who have so obviously done so much to help the Africans, Asian contribution has been indirect and almost incidental.

Thus, the difficulties of the Asians are not merely that they have to revise their own attitudes and behaviour; but also that they have to overcome a huge prejudice on the part of the Africans. Their sincere and conscientious efforts at reconciliation are liable to be looked at askance. The process of adjustment cannot be an entirely one-sided one; though most of the effort must be made by the Asians, the Africans must also indicate that they have an understanding of the dilemmas of the Asians and sympathy for their efforts.

In the light of these attitudes, what are the prospects of Asians successfully dealing with their problems? First, we must look at the adaptive equipment of the Asians. It is obvious that here they have many advantages: they have wealth, education, an adaptability which is often characteristic of immigrants, an increasing awareness of the dilemmas that face them. By the laws of these countries they have a certain status, and the African leaders have by the tone of their speeches tried to reassure the immigrants of a decent future. The provisons for the acquisition of citizenship of these countries are extremely generous for the immigrants. Before the independence of East African countries, there was no such thing as a local citizen-ship. Most of the people living in East Africa were British or British protected subjects, and on that basis, entitled to a legal status in the country.

With the independence of Tanganyika, the question of a Tanganyika citizenship was discussed, mainly in relation to the immigrant races, for the indigenous population would automatically become Tanganyika citizens. Liberal provisions were inserted in the constitution which granted independence; these provisions have acted as the model for Uganda and Kenya on their independence, and thus the provisions in these countries are very similar, except that Kenya is more generous than the others in one or two respects. Basically, in each country, it is provided that anyone born in the country, one of whose parents was also born in the country, and who on the date of independence was a British citizen or protected person, automatically becomes a citizen. Many Asians in East Africa thus automatically became citizens of the countries in which they lived.

Another mode of acquiring citizenship is by registration. It was felt that there were many immigrants in these countries who would not automatically get citizenship, but who had such a connection with these countries that there ought to be some provision for them to acquire citizenship. It was therefore decided that such persons should be allowed to register as citizens, but that they should have to make up their minds to opt for local citizenship within a specified period—the specified period in each country being two years from the time of independence. People who qualify for citizen-ship by registration are those who were born in the country but fail to acquire automatic citizenship because neither of their parents was born in the country. Also included in this category are persons who on the date of independence are citizens of the U.K. and colonies, having acquired this status by naturalization or registration in the country of East Africa whose citizenship they seek. In Kenya, but not in the other countries, there is an additional category: all persons who are cizitizens of the U.K. and colonies and the Republic of Ireland on the day of independence, and who were ordinarily and lawfully resident in Kenya. Again, in Kenya but not elsewhere, citizenship by naturalization is provided for in the constitution—the requirements for eligibility are not too onerous and would cover most Asians who would not become citizens automatically or by registration. Parliaments of Tanganyika and Uganda have been authorized to provide for naturalization, but the right to naturalization does not enjoy constitutional entrenchment as in Kenya. Finally, all persons born after the date of independence, unless they happen to be children of diplomats, automatically acquire the citizenship of the country of their birth.

Dual citizenship is not allowed; if those who become citizens automatically or by registration do not renounce any other citizenship they may have within a specified period, their local citizenship lapses. There are also provisions for the deprivation of citizenship except for 'automatic citizenship'. In Kenya, the power of deprivation can only be exercised in a defined number of cases; in Tanganyika and Uganda there would appear to be no restriction on the power of the legislature to provide for the deprivation of citizenship except that they cannot deprive of his citizenship a person who gets it by virtue of his birth.

From the foregoing account of the provisions about citizenship, it is obvious that most Asians living in East Africa could have obtained an East African citizenship. However, large numbers of them did not opt for such citizenship. This has been partly as a result of much confusion and misunderstanding about the implications of citizenship. Primarily, the decision to retain British or Indian citizenship has been inspired by fear that to give this up would be to give up the right to any kind of protection in the event of confiscation of property or persecution. Also, rumours have been current that once a person gives up his foreign passport he would not be allowed to go abroad, or at least not without the payment of a substantial sum of money.

If the Asians want to stay in East Africa, they have done themselves enormous harm by their hesitance about the question of the acquisition of an East African citizenship. The Africans have come to look upon the scale of Asian acquisition of citizenship as an index of their sincerity and acceptance of African rule; indeed, it is an indication of a firm commitment to East Africa. A careful weighing of the advantages and disadvantages of acquiring these new citizenships is no doubt both wise and reasonable; but to the African this smacks too much of the qualities for which he dislikes the Asians: opportunism, selfishness, wanting the best of all worlds, the obligations of none. Quite apart from damaging their image and failing to present impressive evidence of their sincerity and extent of commitment to East Africa, the Asians have weakened their legal position to fight against discrimination. Discrimination on the basis of colour is rightly open to attack; discrimination on the basis of citizenship, however, is perfectly justifiable, and is indeed usual all over the world. If the Asians want to claim equality of rights and opportunities with the Africans they can only do so on the basis of a common citizenship. To some extent Asian political impact depends on how many Asians take out citizenship, for franchise is quite naturally confined to citizens. Also, some of the rights and freedoms that the minorities were able to write in the constitutions of Uganda and Kenya are confined to citizens. However, a few of the more important rights are not so confined. Thus, the protection to property owners against confiscation without good cause and prompt payment of compensation extends to all owners; the freedoms of expression, association and religion, including the right to establish and maintain institutions for religious and cultural instruction, are guaranteed to all. Thus, in Uganda and Kenya at least, the Asians have security not only against arbitrary deprivation of property, but also an assurance of the right to maintain their distinct cultural institutions.

However, these safeguards seem less important when one considers the security of the right to reside in East Africa of those Asians who do not take the citizenship. In Kenya, the two-year period of grace is not yet over, in Uganda it has just expired, and in Tanganyika it ran out some time ago. Therefore, we might once again turn to the Tanganyika position as a guide to the possible future position throughout East Africa; Uganda now has broadly similar legislation. In Tanganyika, it is now provided by legislation that no non-citizen (except an African from a few neighbouring countries) can enter or remain in Tanganyika without an entry permit. There are two kinds of entry permits—Class A and Class B; the former kind of permit may be granted without the requirement of security, while Class B permit can only be granted on the furnishing of security sufficient to cover the cost of returning him to his country of origin or, in the discretion of the immigration officer, to some other country into which he may be admitted, together with a further sum not exceeding 25 per centum of such first-named sum. People who are initially granted a B class permit can apply for an A class permit, and indeed have to obtain one after the lapse of the period specified in their B class permit. Persons who held certificates of permanent residence are given an A class permit on application within six months; those permits are valid for two years.

The permits, except in the case of the former holders of certificates of permanent residence, are issued subject to conditions relating to the area within which the holder may reside, the occupation or business (if any) in which he may engage, and the restrictions, prohibitions or limitations subject to which he may engage therein; the permits also specify the duration of his residence in Tanganyika. Over and above all this, the permits are liable to be cancelled at the discretion of the immigration authorities, after confirmation by the minister. This machinery enables the government to exercise effective control over the numbers, location and occupation of the immigrants. It also means that Asians who are not citizens have little security of the right to reside in the country. So far there have not been any evictions of Asians, but it is not difficult to imagine that unless race relations improve, the government may feel compelled to resort to its power to expel Asians. The Kenya Government is constitutionally prohibited from expelling anyone, citizen or not, who was ordinarily and lawfully resident in Kenya on the date of independence. If Kenya wants to copy the Tanganyika legislation, a constitutional amendment would be necessary.[5]

The African leaders have tried to reassure the immigrants that they have a future in East Africa, that they would be given equal rights and opportunities. Some Asians remain unconvinced, partly because the words and acts do not always coincide and partly because the salutary effect of a reassuring speech from a minister is quite often offset by violently anti-Asian speeches by some backbenchers who call Asians by such epithets as 'bloodsuckers', 'exploiters', etc. The policy of Africanization of the public services does not tally with assurances of equality and fair policy. This policy is justified on grounds of removing the inequalities of the colonial times.[6] On this basis it must be temporary, and indeed President Nyerere's revocation of this policy in favour of 'localization' has demonstrated the genuineness of this justification, at least in Tanganyika[7].

Nevertheless, the policy of Africanization suffers from some inconsistencies. If its purpose is equalization, then it ought not to be applied as indiscriminately as it has been. As has been shown, it is not the Africans alone who suffered from the colonial system; the Asians suffered as well. There were few Asians in any senior positions in government service. A proper policy of equalization should ensure equality at all levels and this means that some Asians should have been promoted to senior posts in the public service, rather than have an embargo put on their promotion. Not a single permanent secretaryship is held by an Asian in any of the East African governments or in the East African Common Services; and very few indeed are in any senior positions. Many of them are highly qualified and have served their governments with skill and loyalty; they have not been given the recognition they deserve. Nor is any clear indication given as to the criteria to determine when the 'imbalance' has been redressed. This discriminatory practice could, therefore, be carried on well beyond the point justified by the theory of 'imbalance'. It is sometimes not possible to escape the conclusion that the Udoji Commission itself voiced that 'Africanization is not merely a policy of equalization, it is also that all key and policy-advising posts in the Civil Service should be held by Africans'.[8]

The second disquiet about Africanization is the fear that it may generate a momentum that may be beyond the power of the governments to check, once they decide the time has come to put a stop to this policy. The backbench and trade union pressure is too often irresistible. Tanganyika which has a strong, one-party government, had difficulties in substituting localization for Africanization, and it is still doubtful whether localization has now been implemented in practice. The Asians are thus afraid that even given the genuineness of the justification of the policy by the leaders, they might find they are unable to control its momentum. This paragraph points out an important factor in the adjustments of minority-majority relations. It is that the process of adjustment cannot be entirely one-sided. African attitudes will affect the rate and nature of adaptations. More will be said about this factor later.

Against this background of problems, attitudes and prejudices, what are the prospects for the future? What role is the Asian community going to play in East Africa, what is its relationship with the Africans likely to be? It is now accepted by all thinking persons that the Asians 'will have to achieve integration with the Africans'. Unfortunately there has not been much discussion of the meaning of integration. Clearly integration means a *modus vivendi*, a relationship in which the hostility towards the immigrants diminishes or disappears, the immigrants are able to play a meaningful and purposeful part in the country on a basis of equality, and are accepted as full members of the society. As a minimum, this demands from the immigrants an acceptance of and loyalty to the political and civic institutions of the country; it also demands sympathy for the basic aspirations of the majority groups. On the part of the majority group, it calls for tolerance and understanding. What else is essential?

The answer to this question depends on the kind of integration that is sought, and it is here that the need for sharper definitions becomes clear. Students of minority-majority relationships have stated that integration can be achieved by two basic methods—pluralism (sometimes used synonymously with accommodation) or assimilation.[9] Pluralism means a continuation of the minority as a distinct unit within the larger society, community consciousness remains. It implies several areas of life where diversity is tolerated and indeed encouraged, though conformity in some areas is necessary. Areas where diversity is permitted are in personal and family life—religion, culture, marriage, food, etc., and possibly in social institutions, e.g., clubs, societies. A pluralistic society is therefore one in which the minority groups accept the political and civic institutions of the majority group and are sympathetic to its basic aspirations; in return, the majority group tolerates and accepts some of the distinct cultural traits of the minorities, allows them the establishment and maintenance of cultural and social institutions, and enables them to participate in the apparatus of the state on a basis of equality. A successful state of pluralism implies a process of balancing—the conformities that are essential with the diversities that may be permitted. It is also a potentially unstable state; it presupposes that each group is satisfied with its social, economic and political status, and any dissatisfaction in any of these areas is liable to upset the delicate balance. If, as is obvious, the Asians want pluralism, they will not only have to identify the areas where conformity is essential and try to conform, they will also have to help Africans achieve their aspirations in economic and social matters.

Assimilation, on the other hand, is a much more radical process. It rules out all diversities; the end product of assimilation is a situation of complete conformity at all levels of life. The resultant conformity is not an amalgam, but is assimilation to the culture of the dominant group. It implies the disappearance of minorities as distinct units in the society; it presupposes either one or both of the following factors—a decline in the group loyalty and sentiment of the minority and a willingness to abandon its special characteristics in favour of those of the majority, and, on the part of the majority, a determination not to permit the existence of 'distinct pockets' of population and to exact conformity. Above all, it implies basic homogeneity in the society of the majority group, and a belief in its superiority and in the necessity of assimilation. Its demands are primarily on the minority—it calls for radical adjustments by them, but little by the majority, except to permit assimilation.

If Asians are to achieve integration with the Africans, through which of the two paths must they achieve this? The Asian bias is for pluralism. They have accepted African political victory, and the new political and civic institutions. Beyond this they would prefer not to change. As far as the Africans are concerned, their preference is not so obvious. What they have made clear are some of the conditions that are prerequisite to any integration—acceptance of and respect for the new leadership and institutions, loyalty to the country (as evidenced by investing locally rather than sending money abroad), economic help to Africans, especially in the establishment of an African mercantile class. It is not clear whether, given that Asians satisfy these conditions, the Africans will accept their right to be different and yet to participate in the affairs of state. Occasionally, some African leaders have asked for more—e.g., they have asked that the social barriers must come down, as signified by interracial marriages. Others have shown no marked preference for this degree of social integration, and it is significant that the rising African élite prefer to socialize *inter se;* they prefer to marry girls of their own tribe. It is therefore difficult to say whether the Africans want total assimilation. Of course, one difficulty is the lack of a defined, homogenous culture to which assimilation might be effected. African way of life is itself undergoing far-reaching changes, and as has been pointed out above, in the absence of a stable, dominant culture, assimilation is not very practicable. Moreover, in any given situation, the issues are seldom so stark and opposed as assimilation or pluralism. What is more profitable is to try a breakdown of the various areas of relationships—political, economic, social—and to see the degree of assimilation or pluralism demanded or allowed, and the directions in which the developments may take place.

The Tanzania Government is the one which comes nearest to

asking for assimilation. It has frequently attacked communal cultural and social institutions; stopped radio broadcasts in Indian languages; insisted on active Asian participation in local self-help schemes; asked Asians to join TANU, the political party. It is this aspect of her policy which often gives the impression that Tanzania is being hard on its minorites. It may well be that in the long run this kind of forced integration is the best policy as far as the Asians are concerned. Uganda offers a sharp contrast to Tanzania; it is most tolerant of Asians as a separate community; not many anti-Asian speeches are made, nor much advice handed out to them. Uganda Radio offers a few hours per week of Indian programmes; Kenya's position is the least clearly defined; the leaders have talked a great deal of assimilation to 'the African way of life' but the Voice of Kenya continues with its numerous hours daily of Indian programmes. Communal institutions flourish; no efforts have been made to get the Asians involved in political parties or schemes of self-help; women and youth organizations have not become multi-racial.

Politics
It is difficult to analyse the role of the Asians in the political field, in view of the rapidly changing nature of politics. One thing is certain: if the Asians can integrate effectively at the political level, then many of their social and economic problems will be dealt with more sympathetically and successfully. Whatever happens, the loss in the political, unlike the economic, field is likely to be small, for there is so little to lose. One immediate loss, moreover, is that vast numbers of Asians have become disenfranchised after independence. During the British régime, franchise was not related to citizenship (in any case there was no such thing as an East African citizenship), but to residence. There were no fancy educational or property restrictions on the franchise, and so most Asian adults had a vote. But it is doubtful if the vote gave Asians much power. The representation in the legislature was on a communal basis; the Asian representation was at all times a small one, and for years the legislatures were undemocratic and non-responsible. The Asians, therefore, never had any real political power. There are, however, certain consequences of the communal representation that ought to be mentioned. It generated a measure of political consciousness and encouraged communal political organizations. In the early days of East Africa's history, it threw up leaders who were prepared to fight for the African as well. Also, it caused splits in the Asian community, for the Muslims won separate represen-

tation after Indian independence; and the sub-groups in the Asian community tended to put up rival candidates. The disunity caused by this system of communal representation had the serious consequence that the Asian community was unable to formulate a joint, coherent and consistent policy *vis-à-vis* African nationalism. Communal representation produced some psychological satisfaction at the thought that there were in high places members of the community who would look after their interests and make representation to the authorities when the Asians were badly done by; institutionalized protests could be made through the political organizations. All this kept alive a feeling of political identity, rather, identities, and encouraged the formation of political parties and a minimal effort at the formulation of political policies.

With the disappearence of communal representation, a distinctively Asian political contribution must also disappear, and with it very likely Asian activity or even interest in politics. Most Asian political parties have dissolved themselves. There is already apathy, born out of the feeling that the Asians have not got the ability to make a difference in the political set-up. There is of course nothing to prevent the Asian competing in the political arena on the basis of a universal adult franchise. There are few areas of such intense Asian population concentration that a candidate could hope to win an election on the strength of Asian votes alone, and if there were one or two such successful Asian candidates, their say in the councils of the party would be small. East African politics are now basically the politics of parties. Unless an Asian politician has the backing of the major political party in the country, he is unlikely to make any impact. In any case in such circumstances there will be such marked dependence on African support that the majority of the Asians are not likely to have much faith in him as a guardian of Asian interests. There is an acute dilemma for the Asian politician. He is entirely dependent on the African party leaders for his survival and promotion. He cannot, therefore, stand as champion of the Asian cause. Certainly pronouncements in public in favour of such a cause will be few and far between. Even if the African leaders want an Asian to occupy a seat in the legislature and the party council, they would and could hardly allow him to become a public spokesman for the Asians. On the other hand the Asians will cease to regard him as their leader, and continue to feel that there is little future for an independent-minded politician. The Asian politician's influence will be great or small as the African politicians let it. He certainly will have no effective base to work from. If he disagrees with the party policy, he can only hope to change it by persuasion; if he cannot do this, he must either swallow his opposition or go into wilderness.

Therefore to a large extent the future of Asian politicians depends on how effectively they can enter the political parties and get their backing. At one time the major African political parties did not admit non-Africans to membership; this is not so now, and all citizens can join the major political parties. There are a few Asians today who are prominent members of these political parties, these are the people who had the courage to stand out for the African cause during the nationalist struggle. How easy will it be for the younger Asians to acquire a position in the parties?

It is not an easy question to answer for few able young Asians have tried to acquire position of influence in the party. As long as the rewards in politics are as attractive as they are now, an effective Asian entrance will be difficult. Also, with the two or more party system, the Asians will have difficulty in getting into positions of influence in the party; the party which allows them such positions becomes vulnerable to attacks on the ground that it is not primarily concerned with African interests. But the trend in the countries of East Africa is towards a one-party system. In such a system there is either in law or in practice one effective political party which controls most institutions of the state and the instrumentalities of propaganda. Free from fears of rival political parties, the leaders in such a system can impose on the country decisions that may otherwise be politically risky. Theoretically such a system should be more favourable to the Asian politicians than the two-party system; and also to the Asian population in general. In a two-party system, it is difficult for the Asians to decide which party to support; whichever party they do not support, threatens them with all kinds of reprisals. As the Asians in East Africa have generally been divided in their support between the two parties in a particular country, they have become the target of abuse and threats from both the sides. A one-party system eliminates the need for this agonizing decision; the Asian loyalties to the political system can be manifested more readily and fearlessly, and this in part explains the Asian participation in Tanganyika, which is more marked there than in any other East African country.

Moreover this theoretical proposition may not work out— the single party is seldom as monolithic as it seems, and it could be disastrous for the Asians to get involved in the subterranean struggle for power within the single party. On balance, it might be best for the Asians to stand clear of all politics. But the African leaders will not be content with this neutral attitude. On the other hand, it will be difficult for Asians to build a political following. They cannot, however, expect to get into the councils of the party because they can convince the African leadership of their loyalty and ability. They must try to build a grass-roots support; they must be prepared to go out to the small villages and towns in remote parts of the country to address political meetings; they must work for the party at the local and the regional levels. Only if they do this do they have a claim and an opportunity to influence the political decisions in the country. But whether this measure of political integration can be achieved is extremely doubtful. The new political systems in East Africa are certainly not moving towards greater tolerance of diversity; the one-party régimes inevitably lead to demands for increasing conformity, not merely political, but also social and cultural. In this context, the Asians will have to tread extremely carefully. They will have to support the party as a unit, without getting involved in the factions. This will mean that they will not be able to play a very active or influential part in the party; but perhaps salvation for them lies in this posture.

Economics

In many ways the economic problems of Asian-African relationship are the most crucial. In an earlier chapter mention has been made of these problems. They are crucial primarily because they relate to the main field of Asian activity—commerce—and also because some African leaders have made Asian attitude and behaviour in this matter the test of Asian loyalty. Asian dominance of the commerce of East Africa, especially in the retail trade, is responsible in great part for African hostility to the Asians, and unless steps are taken quickly to promote an African mercantile class, this Asian dominance will generate further hostility. If the Asians do not, of their own accord, help the Africans in this matter, the governments are bound to. Under the circumstances, it would be extremely unwise of the Asians not to initiate schemes of help.

How can the Asians help the Africans? The most obvious and easy way is by giving advice and training. The Asians have not done enough in this, but are now beginning to[10]. The Africans have demanded more than advice and instruction; they have asked for loans, goods on easy and long credits, and to be taken into partnerships. For several reasons, the Asians regard these demands as excessive. They do not mind giving loans and credit-terms to African traders, but need to be satisfied of their credit-worthiness. African traders have not so far been conspicuously successful, and from a business point of view, their credit-worthiness, in the majority of cases, is rightly suspect. Many of the discriminatory practices of which the Asian wholesale and retail merchants have been accused are quite rationally based on the relative credit-worthiness of the African and Asian traders. Businessmen everywhere tend to be hard-headed, and when criticizing the attitude of the Asian traders, it is as well to remember that they are asked to be extraordinarily altruistic. The Asian traders, must, however, appreciate the political implications of the matter, especially the fact that the future of the Asians will continue to be precarious till there is a more equitable redistribution of wealth. By trying to hold on to their dominance of commerce, they significantly prevent this redistribution. Perhaps the governments can help by guaranteeing the repayment of loans and credits given to aspiring African traders. Asian traders must appreciate that their relations with aspiring African traders cannot be based purely on principles of sound commercial practice. It is also a political—and some would even say, a moral—question.

As the African mercantile class gains experience and success, the Asians will readily give them loans and credits. But it is doubtful if they will ever find it possible to take on Africans as partners. An African coming in as a partner does not as a rule bring capital, experience or skill with him. He may bring some political security— consideration much more important for the big commercial and industrial firms than for the small *dukawallas*. The big firm thus buys political goodwill by taking on Africans as directors. They are in a much better position to do this than small firms; they are run on modern, expert lines with proper accounts, etc. and have enough income to support African directors and partners. The small firms, on the other hand, are run on very haphazard lines, are generally one-family shows, with accounts in Indian vernaculars which are often intelligible only to the person who writes them. Most of the workers are members of the family or close relatives who put in long hours, take almost no holidays, and earn small wages; the Asian employees of these firms are exploited in a real sense of the term. It is doubtful if many Africans would welcome participation on these terms.

It would thus appear that despite the urgency and seriousness of the problem, the Asian response is not going to be adequate. Eventually, an African mercantile class will grow, but little thanks to the established Asian trading community. By responding so inadequately, the Asians will lose a great opportunity; but an adequate response implies radical transformations in the social structures of the Asian community, with its basic unit, the family. To the Asian traders themselves, mistakenly or not, an adequate response implies an act of self-destruction.

As has been discussed in Chapter 4, the economic future for the Asians is none too bright. They are being steadily pushed out of retail and wholesale trade; they are being sacked from the civil service; private firms are reluctant to take them in their employment. No alternative arrangements are being made to find employment for such persons. Asians with mobility, who almost by definition are the people desperately wanted in East Africa, are leaving for overseas. Many Asians hold British passports which allow them unrestricted entry into Britain; it is clear that large numbers of them will take advantage of this to migrate to Britain. At home, the answer to their economic ills perhaps lies in turning to industrialization, but industrialization requires pooling of resources and the abandonment of many of the old attitudes and so might be difficult to achieve.

One other aspect of economic relations deserves brief discussion— trade unionism. Though one of the earliest trade unionists in East Africa was an Indian, Makhan Singh, Asian participation in the trade union movement is small. Like everything else during the colonial régime, trade unions were organized on a racial basis, with only the African trade unions taking an active part in the nationalist struggle. Since independence, the trade unions have not been integrated. On the other hand, they are effective pressure groups and exert considerable influence. Of all the political forces in East Africa, they tend to be among the most racial-minded, and would certainly oppose any concession to the non-black citizens. For purely economic reasons, the Asians ought to try to get into the trade union movement. As it is, the Asians have little bargaining power (e.g. the incident of mass resignation from EACSO)[11]. It is only if they are effectively organized, with a strong body to back them, that they can hope to secure better working conditions. This will also enable them to manifest their support for fellow African workers, and this in turn will help place the racial factor in proper perspective. It may also make the trade unionists revise their views on a non-discriminate and total Africanization. Growing numbers of Asians are becoming workers and will continue to do so due to the reasons outlined in the chapter on the economic survey, and their effective entry into the trade union movement will help produce racial integration at lower levels of society—in contrast to the cocktail integration which Mboya so derides.

Social

Social relations can be subdivided into various parts, ranging from behaviour to a domestic servant to interracial marriages. As stated earlier, there are some attitudes the Asians will have to revise; they must forget their racial arrogance; they must be more courteous and polite to the Africans. What else? Neither side has evinced any great desire for close social interracial relationships. There are, of course, economic barriers; workers and industrialists do not socialize as a rule, even if they are of the same colour. Disparities in economic means no doubt act as a brake on interracial social relations. There is, however, a rapidly growing class of African elite—politicians, civil servants, professionals—but they do not seem anxious for interracial social contacts. It is possible that they wish to cut non-Africans off from their intimate social circle as a reaction against the previous racial arrogance of the other groups.

Is the pattern of interracial social relations to remain as it is—a superficial mixture at the top, at official and semi-official functions, with little contact at the lower income level groups? As has been mentioned earlier, no group is keen on increased contacts, least of all the Asians. But there are many forces at work which would lead to the breakdown of isolations. Though the residential areas of townships are still segregated (no longer by law, however) the African élite is leaving the 'African locations' and moving into European and upper class Asian areas. If the Asians make the adjustments in the political and economic fields that have been outlined, their conservative, rigid social patterns are bound to undergo important changes. But the most significant factors are at work at the newly integrated kindergartens, schools, universities, hospitals. It will be some time before the effect of these factors becomes obvious (and to some extent the social prejudice at home will counteract the liberalizing influence of interracial contacts at schools), but schools are notoriously effective 'melting pots', and could bring about fundamental changes in the social relations between the races. It is well to point out that the significance of interracial schools is that they bring people of different race together when they are children. University colleges also bring different races together, but at a stage in their life when their racial prejudices are set and difficult to revise. The colleges of the University of East Africa provide instructive examples of the problems and success of interracial living. These colleges are non-racial, bringing together the young men and women of the three races, and are for the most part residential. It cannot be said that these colleges have produced a generation of young people free from prejudice or ignorance. Many visitors to these colleges remark on the voluntary segregation of the races—in the libraries, dining halls and cafeteria, each race forms its own clusters. The colleges have not so far significantly helped in promoting racial harmony; but of course, they have been going as interracial institutions only for a few years.

The experience in the University colleges illustrates the point that, in the short run, increased social contacts will create more problems than they will solve. The bitterness of past feelings, the prejudices, come to the fore. Students of one race display astonishing ignorance of the social conventions of students of another race; such is the state of race relations in East Africa. This ignorance produces great tensions, causes misunderstandings, results in people taking umbrage when no offence is intended. People coming from different backgrounds and customs (and even values) are expected to lead a communal life on a residential campus for well over half the year; because they lack knowledge about the ways of life and thought of the other races, the process of settling down to a communal life is never free from friction. The result is often the segregated pattern of student life that one sees in the colleges. Given some knowledge of the ways of life of the other races, much of the friction could be avoided.

The experience of racial living in the colleges illustrates the difficulties of social relationships, and also that unless these difficulties are successfully resolved, the races will retire to their separate groups. It is therefore essential not only to provide opportunities for racial contacts, but also to ensure that people of one race are given some knowledge of the customs of others. Unless the problem is carefully tackled, the result might be much greater harm through rushed programmes. People have said that racial marriages are the answer to racial problems. There is a certain naiveté in this view, for not only can a few racial marriages exacerbate feelings unless there is general approval of racial marriages in the communities concerned, but also because racial marriages are not the solution, but evidence of successful solution of the problems. They presuppose some knowledge and understanding of the other partner's race, and a willingness to accept its ways. This is why a crashed programme of racial marriage cannot be the solution to the racial problems but only evidence that the problems are being successfully tackled.

It does seem as if the social pattern of relationships will not change much for some time to come. This in itself will not harm the future of Asians, so long as the present coincidence of class and wealth changes. With prosperous African middle and upper classes, we may reach a state of stability, where social diversities are accepted within a wider framework of political and economic integration.

Conclusion

The problems of adjustments and adaptations that the Asians face are thus quite difficult. Will the Asians successfully make the necessary revisions? It is not easy to answer this question. Most Asians think that they have no future in East Africa; they feel that race is too fundamental a factor in East African relationships, and that no measure of integration will help the Asians; the Arabs in Zanzibar, they might well say, achieved a remarkable degree of integration (religious, linguistic, cultural) with the Africans, but this did not avail them at the time of the 1964 revolution. High expectations have been generated in East Africa; clearly there will be many failures and setbacks in the realization of these expectations. Will the Asians not become scapegoats?

I feel that a more optimistic prediction would be justified, without minimising the great force of racialism. The Asian community seems to be coming round to the view that they have to stay in East African; emigration, at best, is a partial answer. Therefore, there are the beginnings of a drastic revision of attitudes. Moreover, the younger generation of Asians, born and bred in East Africa, has no other home and knows no other loyalties. The contrast between the younger and the older Asians is striking; in many Asian families there have been fundamental clashes between the younger and the older members on attitudes to African nationalism, producing tensions and bitterness. The younger Asians have tried to convince their elders that the Africans are capable of colour-blindness and magnanimity to a degree that the Asians and Europeans were not. These younger Asians have yet to be accepted fully by the Africans; they have been isolated from their own community, but have not yet found new moorings. Some of them, simplifying the issues by thinking that their loyalty ought to be rewarded, are beginning to feel frustrated. They have an important part to play in promoting racial understandings; their disillusionment with African leadership would be a great setback. On the African side, there is bound to arise a new generation on whom there are no scars of racial discrimination and arrogance. They may find it easier to accept the sincerity and loyalty of the immigrant races in a way that the present leadership cannot. The onus of creating better race relations is beginning to shift to the Africans.

Growing prosperity among the Africans will no doubt reduce some of the tensions that are generated by economic disparities, the relationship of master and servant, but which often take racial forms. Mixed schools and other institutions will promote racial understandings. Genuine and unambiguous Asian commitment to the new East Africa could help a lot.

The atmosphere is not unpropitious. True, there has been discrimination in the past against the Asians; but the African leaders have repeatedly said that this is only temporary in order to redress the imbalance of the past. Tanganyika has already ended discrimination.[12] The leaders in all the three countries of East Africa have accepted the ideology of equality and fairness; they have constantly reiterated this in their speeches. Though occasionally they have gone back to the past and pointed out the racial arrogance of the immigrants, they have more often preached the doctrine of let bygones be bygones. They have promised security to the immigrants; and proclaimed their desire to establish model states in East Africa where the different races live together in peace and friendship, on a basis of equality. Thus, the ideological setting for a meaningful integration is there. The governments, with the support of private organizations, have set about dismantling the racial institutions of the past to create true non-racial institutions. An active policy of integration is being pursued—for the first time in the history of East Africa. Thus, while it is quite true that the last sixty years in East Africa produced no integration, it does not follow that the future must be equally bleak.

The philosophy of the states has changed in favour of integration; the governments must now implement this philosophy in a meaningful way; they must accept their responsibility for ensuring equality and justice among all citizens. Meanwhile, one must continue to hope that this great experiment in social engineering will succeed and that Asians will be accepted, and will play a positive role, in the new societies of East Africa.

References

1. The Tanzania Government has recently admitted that Asian entrepreunerial and management skills and capital have not been adequately exploited. In a statement it stressed the need to exploit Asian skills for the success of the Five Year Plan. See *The Nationalist* (Dar es Salaam) March 15, 1965.

2. See Chapter 4 for details of the provisions for this purpose.

3. The system of '*kipande*', a kind of passbook was not introduced in Uganda or Tanganyika.

4. See generally, George Bennett, *Kenya: A Political History* (O.U.P., 1963) Mr. Oginga Odinga has acknowledged this contribution of the Asians. '*Seminar* 1960', (New Delhi).

5. Such an amendment has now been made: Kenya Constitution (Amendment) Act, 1965.

6. The Report of the Africanization Commission for the East African Common Services Organization (The Udoji Commission) 1963, gave some other reasons for the policy of Africanization. (*a*) *Political motivations.* It is embarrassing for the newly independent countries to retain former colonial civil servants. (*b*) *Functional.* Expatriates may leave at short notice, especially as they have an assurance of a handsome compensation; this uncertainty and the turnover of staff makes long-term planning impossible. Africanization ensures permanence and stability in staffing. (*c*) *Economic motivations.* Expatriates are expensive, and they send the money out of the country. Also the employment of expatriates makes it difficult for young countries to devise indigenous and realistic salaries and conditions of service related to the productive capacity of the country rather than to the prevailing world market conditions from which expatriates are recruited. (*d*) *Social and long-term motivations.* When an expatriate retires and leaves the country, he takes his experience with him. With African civil servants, on the other hand, their

accumulated knowledge and experience could be placed at the disposal of the community in various capacities.

None of these reasons should lead to the exclusion of Asian citizens from employment in the civil service.

7. See footnote 12.

8. Op. cit., p. 11.

9. On this question, see a UNESCO study edited by W. D. Borrie, *The Cultural Integration of Immigrants* (Paris, 1959), especially Chapter IV.

10. E.g. towards the end of 1964, the (Asian) Dar es Salaam Merchants Chamber announced a comprehensive scheme to accelerate the participation of Africans in the commercial and industrial sectors of the economy, through loans, partnerships, and training in commercial techniques.
    The Nationalist (Dar es Salaam) 17th August, 1964.

11. In 1963 hundreds of Asian EACSO employees handed in their resignation on hearing rumours to the effect that their terms of service were to be altered to their disadvantage. They later repented of their haste and tried to withdraw their resignation, but the Organization refused to take them back.

12. In January 1964 President Nyerere ordered the end of discrimination. He said, 'We cannot allow the growth of first and second class citizenship. Both as a matter of principle and as a matter of common sense, discrimination against certain Tanganyika citizens, on grounds of origin must go. There can be no more prevarication.' The *Tanganyika Standard*, 8th January, 1964.

8 6 7 8 0

Published by Oxford University Press, P.O. Box 12532, Nairobi
and printed in Nairobi by East African Printers Kenya Ltd., Nairobi